A TALE OF TWO VILLAGES

HUTTON AND CRANSWICK

by

Herbert Johnson

Revised edition

HUTTON PRESS
2000

Published by

The Hutton Press Ltd.,
130 Canada Drive, Cherry Burton,
Beverley, East Yorkshire HU17 7SB

Copyright © 2000

No part of this book may be reproduced, stored in a retrieval system, or transmitted in any form, or by means electronic, mechanical, photocopying, recording or otherwise without the prior permission of the Publishers and the Copyright holders.

Printed by: Burstwick Print & Publicity Services,
13a Anlaby Road, Hull. HU1 2PJ

ISBN 1 902709 08 X

CONTENTS

Acknowledgements 5

Foreword 6

Chapter 1 Hutton Cranswick: Village and parish . . . 7

Chapter 2 Hutton Cranswick in the Domesday Book 10

Chapter 3 Life after the Norman Conquest 12

Chapter 4 The 17th and early 18th centuries 14

Chapter 5 The open field system 17

Chapter 6 The Enclosures (1770) 19

Chapter 7 The Turnpike Trusts 25

Chapter 8 Conditions at the end of the 18th century. 28

Chapter 9 The Napoleonic Wars 30

Chapter 10 The early 19th century 33

Chapter 11 Early Victorian days 35

Chapter 12 Life in the middle of the 19th century . . . 37

Chapter 13 Late Victorian and Edwardian days 54

Chapter 14 The rise and fall of the Londesboroughs 79

Chapter 15 From the parish register 83

Chapter 16	Education before 1870	88
Chapter 17	Education Act 1870 and onwards	93
Chapter 18	Cows, pigs and ponds	101
Chapter 19	The first three decades of the 20th century	117
Chapter 20	The hinding and hiring system	127
Chapter 21	The horse on the farm	140
Chapter 22	The Depression years of the 1930s	150
Chapter 23	The Second World War	164
Chapter 24	Post-war changes	171
Chapter 25	Hutton Cranswick Show	173
Chapter 26	Village families	179
Chapter 27	Hutton Church and its bells	185
Chapter 28	Characters : Tales from the past	187
Chapter 29	The East Yorkshire Dialect	192
Chapter 30	Requiem for a village	198
Chapter 31	Postscript	204
Appendix 1	Town and country planning	211
Select Bibliography		214

ACKNOWLEDGEMENTS

An initiative begun by the Committee of the Hutton Cranswick Bulletin. John Forgham, Editor of the bulletin, would like to acknowledge the following people who have made this reprint possible.

Susan Wardell, for organising the creation of the copy.
Mary Mawer, for the original suggestion and her knowledge of the Village.
Les Wilkie, for writing the final chapter.
Joan Wilkie, for the proof reading.
Jean Benn, for her support.
Pauline Forgham, for the coffee.
Beryl Stephenson, for controlling our money.
Norman Smith for the appendix on planning.
Charles Brook, of the Hutton Press for the encouragement.

And all those villagers who searched their lofts and family memorabilia for the photographs used throughout the book.

The following families sponsored the printing of this edition by purchasing advance copies of the book :
Helen Adams; B & A E Allgood; John Angus; M Bahn; Sylvia Baldwin; Jean Benn; C Black; Kate Booth; R F Bradley; D E Butler; Sonia Butler; Ron Collins; Rhoda Consitt; D A Dawe; G & S Dixon; Shirley Doughty; Bill & Lesley Eldridge; D Elliott; R Ellis; L Featherstone; Mrs Foreman; John & Pauline Forgham; Les Frank; Brian Freeman; Adrian Fry; Betty Glocko; D Gowthorpe; Anita & Mike Grace; Mary Joyce Gray; Kathleen Hales; M E Hall; Pam & Keith Harrison; E Hellen; M Heuck; M Hodgson; J M Hooper; Don & Barbara Hutton; R D Jones; R J Kennett; Marjorie Lambourne; Rob & Jane Leonard; Philip Love; S Lowe; Eric Marshall; Niamh Marshall; Mary Mawer; D J Mawson; D K & S McCoy; Gail Newlove; Angela Nickolds; Y Oliver; Stan Oxendale; N Parkin; E J Peck; K D Pickering; Anne & Jeff Pinder; Joan & Tony Pinder; Jo Richards; Gwyneth Richardson; Chris & Val Robson; G Robson; Dr. Mike Rogers; Linda Ross; Angela & Paul Ryan; Mark Scott; P Sherriff; David Shimmin; Gina Simpson; Norman & Jean Smith; A Soloman; D M & G Staples; Beryl Stevenson; N Stuart; Sandra Tarrant; A Ternant; Dr. D Thomas; Val Thompson; E Tomlinson; A Twiddle; Sue Wardell; Brad Webster; J & E Wigham; Joan Wilkie; Carol Wilson.

FOREWORD

From William the Conqueror to the new millennium in 2000, this book documents the development of Hutton Cranswick from two villages, each owned by the Archbishop of York and the King to the current, single, thriving village.

The research and original text of Herbert Johnson has been left largely unaltered and any references to 'current' time were 'current' 20 years ago in 1980.

Les Wilkie, a resident of more than twenty years, who has seen the changes to the village take place up dated the book to the year 2000 by writing chapter 31. The bulletin committee hopes that in twenty years time chapter 32 will be written by an existing resident who, having noted the changes taking place in this growing working village will feel the need to document the changes by reprinting this book. We have added an appendix on planning compiled by Norman Smith, which covers the whole of the 20th Century to the present day.

The world around Hutton Cranswick has seen great change and some momentous events in the last twenty years. The names that will be remembered from this last twenty years include Margaret Thatcher, Terry Waite, Arthur Scargill, Nelson Mandella, Shergar, Robert Maxwell, Mikhail Gorbachov, Yitzhak Rabin, and Bill Gates; whilst the memorable events which will form part of this country's and world history include Privatisation, Labours landslide Victory, the break up of the USSR and the re-unification of Germany. The World has also achieved much; The Channel Tunnel, the ending of the cold war, the Mir Space station, Dolly the Sheep and at the turn of the century the strongest indication of peace in Northern Ireland.

On the blacker side we have seen our share of disasters including, Chernobyl, Lockerbie, Hillsborough, Piper Alfa, The Kings Cross fire, B.S.E, The Zeebruge Ferry disaster, the death of Diana Princess of Wales and theatres of war in many parts of the world.

But the village goes on, believing it is largely unaffected by world events, a microcosm of current English country life. In truth we have all been affected by the changes in the last twenty years, as our ability to contact the world at the touch of a few keys has become a reality. Communication is at the heart of world development and if the developments of the next twenty years are as momentous as the last twenty we will see a very different village in a changed world in 2020.

John Forgham.
Editor Hutton Cranswick Bulletin
Spring 2000

CHAPTER ONE

HUTTON CRANSWICK VILLAGE AND PARISH
WITH SUNDERLANDWICK AND ROTSEA

Here, long before the Normans came
The Anglo-Saxons fought the Danes.
But time and tides have swept along,
And the warriors of those years have long since gone.
Now, in the early days of flaming June
The hawthorns in the hedges bloom.
In July wild roses the roadsides adorn,
And the scent of honeysuckle lingers every dawn.
While in the meadows at your feet,
Grow the golden blossomed meadowsweet.

The village of Hutton was called Huttone in the Domesday Book, though in the seventeenth century it was Huton in the Parish Register. Cranswick was Cransvyric. The two hamlets or townships - as they used to be called - of Rotsea and Sunderlandwick were Rotesse and Sundreslanvick. Hutton is said to be a Danish word meaning 'village on the end of a hill'. According to some historians, Hutton is a place of great antiquity and was at one time a fortified camp where there were fierce battles between the Saxons and the Danes.

Little is known about East Yorkshire villages before the Norman Conquest, unless there was a monastic house which kept a few records. Hutton always seems to have been the smaller of the two villages, as the inhabitants may have drifted down to Cranswick where there was a better water supply. The lower end of Cranswick was, and still is, supplied with natural springs, while Hutton was practically waterless, especially in a dry summer.

Cranswick or Cransvyric (the locals call it 'Cransick') is of Anglo-Saxon origin, and is thought to be associated with cranes. Indeed, there may have been cranes living in the carrs to the east of the village many years ago. Hutton and Cranswick were at one time two separate villages, and up to the Enclosures (1770) there were no houses between the villages. Today, for administrative purposes it is all one village, though until April 1977 each possessed its own Post Office and the addresses differ slightly.

The Green, approximately 6 ½ acres, belonged originally to the Hothams, Lords of the Manor. The villagers' cattle will have grazed the green for centuries just as they did in the early part of the present century. Then, where the children's swings now stand, there was a dilapidated cottage with an orchard. The last tenant was an old man named Matthew Hicks. When he died it was all levelled to the ground. The garden hedges were pulled up and today no trace of it remains. The green, under the Commons Act of 1899, is now designated common land.

In later years the Hutton villagers (they were sometimes called 'Yuttonites') used to joke that though Cranswick had most of the amenities, such as schools, pubs, and railway station, Hutton had the church and the churchyard, and when the Cranswick residents' days were ended they came to stay permanently. As one Huttonian put it: 'If thev niver been straight befoor they are noo'.

Rotsea (Rotesse) at the east side of the parish adjoins the River Hull. The name is supposed to be of Scandinavian origin and may mean 'Lake which contains decayed matter'.

Featherholms nearby has Danish connections, and a similar name (Fyerholm) is to be found in Denmark. It is thought the name arose because great flocks of birds lived in the neighbourhood. Rotsea had a number of duck decoys, as had Leven and other places where there was plenty of water. Tame ducks were trained to attract wild fowl into the narrow end of the decoy where they could be trapped. Watton decoy, not far away, was surrounded by an area of 1,000 acres of marsh and water and sometimes as many as 400 fowl were taken in a day. The decoys disappeared when the carrs were drained in the eighteenth century.

Near the road to Far Rotsea are the remains of an old village. It has been practically levelled in recent times, though forty-five years ago the ruins of the buildings stood about five feet above the ground, and the outline of each could be clearly traced. It appears to have been just a small hamlet, and had a rather larger building that must have been a kind of hall or meeting place. Nothing seems to be known of the people who lived there, or when and why they left. Fish and waterfowl were probably their main means of subsistence, and as these lowlands were drained and cultivated, their livelihood would disappear also. I believe the site is now protected and Hull University is to be allowed the first 'dig', so in time the little hamlet may yield its secrets.

Corpslanding is the name of a single farm standing on the banks of the West Beck, or River Hull, near Rotsea. Its name has never been satisfactorily explained. One historian claims that the name is a combination of Scottish, Swedish and Icelandic. Local tradition has it that a corpse was landed at the wharf. This has been discounted by historians, but since they can be no more sure than the locals, we can take our pick.

The occupier of Corpslanding still pays a small rent to Hutton Cranswick Parish Council for the use of the old wharf site, covering about three acres.

Anlaf's fleet was supposed to have landed here and marched across country the three miles or so to Battleburn, which was said to be the scene of the Battle of Brunanburg, where Athelstan inflicted a great defeat on Anlaf. Whether Battleburn, near Kirkburn, was the scene of the battle of Brunanburg is also doubtful.

Sunderlandwick (Sundreslanvic), meaning 'dairy farm on a separate piece of land' according to G. Ross, was owned by the Anglo-Dane Jarl Siward Digera until his death in York in 1055. In fact, he controlled most of the land on the East Yorkshire coast. He was known as the Unconquerable. When dying of some illness, and being much aggrieved that he could not die in battle, he asked to be dressed in all his battle regalia, and then he passed away content. His name is preserved for posterity in that he, or his namesake, is mentioned in Macbeth.

There is also a lost village at Sunderlandwick, and during the last century a coffin was found which had been scooped out of the trunk of an enormous oak. It was in the form of a huge boat six feet long by four feet broad and contained three skeletons. They were thought to be the remains of a chief and his companions or bodyguards and had lain undisturbed for 2,000 years. In those days of no roads, only mud tracks through the forests and scrub land, the easiest way to the old village would be along the stream now known as Bar Beck. It would also supply them with fish. Today this stream, along with the next one nearer Driffield, is renowned far beyond Yorkshire for the quality of its trout fishing.

CHAPTER TWO

HUTTON CRANSWICK IN THE DOMESDAY BOOK

Game, or Gamel, has eight carucates for geld. There is land for four ploughs. Hugh has a plough there and twelve villeins (villagers or peasant landowners), with four ploughs. It is a league in length and one in breadth. It was worth sixty shillings. It is now worth twenty. The Archbishop of York had land at Huttone, and the King possessed land at Cransvyric.

The lordship of Meaux, near Beverley, was given to one of William the Conqueror's officers named Gamel, who was born at Meaux in Normandy. He made it his seat, and peopled it with his townsmen. Whether this was the same Gamel we do not know, as Gamel seemed to be a common name then.

The Gamel at Cranswick was also the King's theign or thane, i.e. he was a servant of the King or a nobleman. After the Conquest this title was discontinued. It is interesting to note that plough oxen were the only farm stock recorded in the Domesday Book.

Hutton Cranswick Parish

It is a parish of 6,449 acres with Rotsea and Sunderlandwick, and in 1971 the population was 1,163. Most of it is situated on the Hull Valley, which extends roughly from Wansford near Driffield to Hull, and is drained by the River Hull. The western side is practically on the foothills of the Wolds. Some of it extends beyond the disused Market Weighton railway. To the north it is bounded by the trout stream, Bar beck, about half a mile from Driffield. The beck is so called because the toll bar stood near the bridge over the stream. The River Hull is the boundary on the east, and to the south the Watton parish.

The Hull to Bridlington road runs through the western part of the parish and historians tell us that two million years ago the sea came up to where this road now runs. In fact if you drew a line from Flamborough to Hessle, it would follow the chalk cliff of that time. In some places just above Hutton Cranswick village there are nearly thirty feet of impervious clay over the chalk where the chalk cliff has broken down over thousands of years. Thus, much of the parish was originally under water. Most of it is heavy clay land, and some near the River Hull is 'carr' (black soil rather like the Fens).

Before the draining of the Hull Valley towards the end of the eighteenth century, part of the eastern end of the Parish was flooded for the best part of the year. Somewhere in the distant past it must have been well wooded, as large pieces of bog oak are still being ploughed up. A few grass snakes still live in this area. This peaty type of carr land, if it catches fire, can burn for a long time, and it used to be a strict rule never to burn thorns or 'wicks' on this type of land.

CHAPER THREE

LIFE AFTER THE NORMAN CONQUEST, AND THE MIDDLE AGES

The villagers lived in their huts of mud and clay, with thatched roofs, no chimneys and no glass-covered windows. Even in the fifteenth century glass was rare. In 1930 a house was rebuilt in Southgate, Cranswick, and the builders found that nearly all the walls were made of clay.

There are three fields where a great deal of clay has been taken out. The first is the one behind the White Horse, Cranswick, and it is still known as Brickyard Field. The second is one of the Heddlemere fields, near the railway at the end of Station Lane. The third is on the East Side of the railway, near the station. This is also called Brickyard Field. These fields are marked on the Enclosure Map of 1770, yet there is nothing to indicate that bricks were ever made there. There seem to have been only four people engaged in brick making and that was in the 1870's. In the first place the clay was probably dug for constructing the walls of the houses. Clay abounds in this district and the village people had a plentiful supply right under their feet. Then the technique of brick making was developed. Mr Stan Blanchard of Driffield, whose father and grandfather ran the Bridlington Road Brickworks, says this could be quite a simple process. The bricks were placed in a clamp, fired with coal and left to burn for a week. When the brick making ended in that particular field and the grass had grown again, there was nothing to show except a five or six-foot dip in the ground.

Mr Blanchard says there are no records of bricks from their brickworks being used for building Hutton Cranswick houses, though many land drain pipes from there were used to drain the fields in this parish. Two of the fields belonging to the Parish Council were drained with pipes from Blanchard's Brickworks before the First World War.

Brickmaking did not require kilns to be built, and a local bricklayer could buy a piece of land in a field and make his own bricks as he required them. This was the case, for example, with Henry Watson, who in the 1851 census was recorded as the licencee of the 'White Horse' and also a bricklayer. He may have made his own bricks in his own field, the Brickyard Field, behind his premises.

Life was hard for the villagers, and a supply of food came before everything else. Often the stock were killed and eaten at the onset of winter, as the fodder supplies would not last the winter through. In most parishes there was a great deal of common land, where the villagers could graze their stock. Even what was called waste land had its uses, as the swine could forage for food there, and there was also timber for hut building and fuel.

In this parish there were Cranswick Common and Hutton Common on the east of the parish. Some of this land was waterlogged for a greater part of the year, but the villagers could graze their stock on it in summer and there would be wildfowl to catch in the winter. In the Parish Register there is a grassman recorded as living in Sheepman Lane (a grassman is a man who has the right to graze stock on a common).

In most villages there was a pond for the stock and a fishpond. Some of these ponds are very ancient. The one at Wetwang was in existence in 1303, and the two ponds at Hutton, now filled in, may have been excavated when the village consisted of a few huts, possibly as far back as Saxon times. The same could apply to Cranswick.

Most villages were built near a stream. Hutton seems to have been an exception, as the nearest stream, Skerne or Northfield Beck, is nearly a mile away. The Hutton inhabitants, in a dry summer, would probably wash their clothes in this beck.

On the beck bank at Burton Agnes in the seventeenth century there was a 'wash stone' below which nobody could wash 'puddings, fish, clothes or other filthy things'. The clothes were probably washed the same way as the Indians did, by hammering them on a rock. This had prompted Mark Twain to say, when visiting India, that it was the first time he had seen anybody breaking stones with a shirt front.

The plague or Black Death reached England in the fourteenth century and arrived in York in May 1349. There is no record of it in this parish. There are hardly any records of any sort in fact until the seventeenth century. At Meaux Abbey near Beverley, the Abbot and five monks died in a single day. Out of fifty monks only ten survived. At Wharram Percy, just across the Wolds, the population was so reduced that the side aisles of the church were pulled down.

The population of England and Wales in 1457 was roughly between 2 ½ and 3 million. In this parish the number would be somewhere between two to three hundred, though this is more or less a guess. Even at the first census in 1802, there were only 694.

CHAPTER FOUR

THE SEVENTEENTH AND EARLY EIGHTEENTH CENTURIES

The famous, or infamous, Ship Tax levied by Charles the First, enforced despite much opposition until 1641 and one of the causes of the Civil War, was levied on all villages or townships. The villages and hamlets in this parish did not escape:

Hutton Cranswick	£17.	7.	0
Sunderlandwick	£ 2.	10.	0
Rotsea	£ 5.	0.	0

Driffield, though not much bigger than Hutton Cranswick was assessed at £22.5.0d. The money was to go towards building two ships of 480 tons apiece.

The Civil War did not make much difference to the ordinary peasant or villager, even though Marston Moor and the fighting near Hull and Beverley was not so very far away, and the two Hothams, father and son of the local landowning family, were defended by Durant Hotham on a charge of treason.

There is also a local legend that Cromwell once positioned a gun on Barf Hill near Wilfholme and blew part of Watton Abbey down. However, that story may be on a par with a tale of those years when one contryman was telling another that the Royalists and Parliamentarians were fighting. All he got in reply was, "Is them lot at it ageann".

The villager was still very much under the heel of the landowner, and there were no winds of change blowing in his direction. Still, Gerrard Winstanley, a Lancashire man, with some supporters, began to cultivate some waste land near London. He said the common people should have the right to dig, plough, plant or live upon the commons without paying a rent to anyone. In 1652 he submitted a plan to Cromwell for a 'Law of Freedom', in which there would be no lords of manors, lawyers, landlords or tithes. He seems to have been a man very much before his time.

The Justices of the Peace had considerable powers, and were all from the gentry, such as the Hothams, Constables, Legards and Boyntons. Durant Hotham of Lockington, and Thomas Crompton of Sunderlandwick were Justices for this district. Crompton was appointed Justice of the Peace after the Restoration. During the Civil War he was a Royalist and after Parliament conquered Yorkshire he was fined £880, a huge sum in those days.

The Justices had the power to act as a kind of Industrial Relations Court and a carpenter who left his work before it was finished could be sentenced to a month's imprisonment and ordered to pay £5.00. Wages were also fixed by them for mowers, shearers, binders, thatchers and many others.

Malting and brewing were restricted after a bad harvest. This seems quite a reasonable law. After the Civil War no barley was allowed to be used for malting until after Michaelmas. Fines were also imposed on unlicensed premises. Alehouses seemed to have caused the Justices a great deal of trouble, as many of them were unlicensed. In Hutton nearly two hundred years later (1840), there was one inn and two alehouses, which seems a lot for a population of probably 200 or maybe less.

A token was a disc redeemable in lawful money and was often issued when there was a shortage of copper and the Government was not making halfpennies or farthings. In the reign of Charles II there were twenty thousand different types of tokens issued by shopkeepers. These were usually a farthing, halfpenny and penny. As a rule they were only used in the locality where they were issued. Some were given to the poor and needy to exchange for food and drink. Innkeepers issued more tokens than any other tradesmen. Even in the nineteenth century they were still being used, though they had been banned in 1672. Normally a man included his wife's Christian names, putting the initial of the surname in the middle of and above the two Christian name initials as in the halfpenny token of George and Mary Wilberfoss of Cranswick: $G^W_{\frac{1}{2}} M$

On the obverse side of the token were the arms of the Grocer's Company; on the reverse: In Cranswick. 1670. G.W. (George Wilberfoss married Margaret Warton in 1664).

The Hobmans were mentioned in the Parish Register in the seventeenth century. They seem to have owned a considerable amount of property in that and the preceding century and yet by the time of the enclosures they had completely disappeared. Like the Sykes of Sledmere, there were merchants from Hull. Hesketh of London was a master mariner, and another one lived for a time in Danzig in Poland. In some old documents of the seventeenth century there were also Duke, Frances and Randolphus. A Josh Sykes from Hull and Mark Masterman Sykes were some of these.

1611
Duke Hobman owned four cottages, eighty acres of land, twenty of meadow, twenty of pasture, two of wood, furze and heath, and common pasture for all cattle in Cranswick. He also had some cottages in

Southgate.

1674

Mr W Wilkinson was tenant of a house owned by Duke Hobman and he paid a rent of £12 per year, with '12 dozen pigeons, 1 bushel of apples and two pecks of pears'. W. Wilkinson's rent would be fairly high judged by the standards of that time, especially with the mixed bag of pigeons, apples and pears.

1686

Two Jenkinsons (father and son) sold five cottages to Hesketh Hobman for £100. Descendants of the Jenkinsons, originally from Lund, still existed 100 years later, and were classed as yeomen. Hobman Lane must have got its name from the long departed Hobman family, though it is known locally as 'Oggleman'.

CHAPTER FIVE

THE OPEN FIELD SYSTEM

Previous to enclosing in this parish there were very few enclosed fields. Most of these were in the village, where the stock were brought in at night. The rest of the parish was open fields. Here are some of the field names: East Fields, West Fields, North Fields, Gosberdale, Priest Ings, Little Wotherams and Heddlemere.

East Fields and West Fields were both to the east of Cranswick village. North Fields was to the north of Hutton and Priest Ings were near Sheepman Lane, where the railway now runs. The aerodrome was built on Little Wotherams. Gosberdale was on the east side of what is now Eastfield Farm, and Heddlemere just to the north of Cranswick. Most of these were open fields until 1770. Some were just common land, so we get Cranswick Common, and the land bordering Corpslanding Road was Hutton Common.

Every parish had its quota of moor or common. This was usually the wettest or the worst land to cultivate, and provided the villagers with grazing for their stock, as it had done for centuries. When there was so much open field, all grazing, cutting hay etc had to conform to certain rules, and these were enforced by a majority of the villagers. In some cases fines were imposed on those who transgressed. The stock were tended by a cowherd, or 'cootenther' on the common or open fields and brought home to the village at nightfall. Incidentally, the name cowherd was still being used in the middle of the nineteenth century when a Seth Walker, twelve years old, hired at Southall, was described as such.

A lot of the land in this parish seems to have been landed up for drainage long before the Enclosures were ever thought of. There seems to have been a vast block of land landed up, rig and forr (ridge and furrow), bordering 'Corpslanding' Road (Hutton Common). The lands (with furrows), most of them about twelve to fourteen yards wide, would serve the dual purpose of drainage and boundary markers.

At first glance the road looks as though it has been taken over the lands, as they can be traced on both sides of the road, and they run from south to north. The same applies to Southburn Road, though some of it has been levelled up by building spoil. The road which runs to Corpslanding wharf on the West Beck must have been in existence a long time as river traffic was used a great deal when the roads were practically impassable in winter. My own theory is that this road was, at one time, the headland where the ploughs turned round. So some ploughman, centuries ago, with a straight eye, and a rudimentary plough with a team of oxen may have 'yarked out' (made a straight mark on) those headland marks, to give us the boundaries of a modern road.

In some parishes there were six bylawmen, as well as one or two constables. Meetings were sometimes called by the pinder who seems to have been an important man. His job was to impound all straying stock. The local pinfold extended from the bottom of Hutton Road (at one time called Towns Road), and across to the Hull/Driffield road (about two acres in all), just behind the house and buildings belonging to Miss G Berriman. (Part of the Green was once used as a pinfold). There the stock would have to stay until claimed by the owner, who had to pay a fine. Sometimes the pinder was paid so much a head, in other parishes he received a yearly sum.

That was the picture in the middle of the eighteenth century; a more or less self contained community. There were cobblers, tailors, joiners, blacksmiths, hawkers and the village shopkeepers supplying most of the needs of the people. Hutton Cranswick at this time had 148 families. Hutton had 43 houses, and Cranswick 80, there were no buildings in between the villages. The inhabitants may have numbered 400 - 500, but the population of the country was growing. At this time it had reached about seven million in England and Wales, and more food was needed to feed the increasing number of urbanites. However, an event was approaching which would change the whole face of the countryside - The Enclosures, and not always to the benefit of the rural dweller.

CHAPTER SIX

THE ENCLOSURES (1770)

The man behind the Enclosures was Arthur Young, the Secretary of the first Board of Agriculture in England. He was also a failed farmer, but gave good and practical advice to the farmers of his day. He probably benefited by the mistakes he made, and knew many of the pitfalls to avoid. We seem to have a parallel in modern times, as some of the advisers in the old War Ag. of wartime memory, were bankrupt farmers. Young was a great advocate of the Enclosure system, and of the idea that smallholdings should be made into larger ones. Now, just over 200 years later, we hear the same cry, regardless of the fact that the smaller farms usually produce more per acre.

*HUTTON CRANSWICK PARISH ENCLOSURES,
12TH SEPTEMBER 1769.*

> The Commissioners appointed by an Act of Parliament for dividing the open arable fields, meadow grounds, commons, pastures and commonable lands within the township of Hutton Cranswick, in the East Riding, do hereby give notice that they intend to meet at the house of Richard Scales in Hutton Cranswick, on Wednesday the 13th day of September at nine-o-clock in order to receive the claims the Commissioners intend upon the valuation of lands within the said township.
> Commissioners for the Enclosures were :
> John Outram, John Bains and George Jackson.
> Enclosure map drawn up by Peter Nevill, Beningholme Grange, 1770
> Enclosure award April 12th 1771.

The roads were also to be staked out 60 feet wide, though some are slightly over. The Road boundaries were often defined by a plough furrow. Could it have been that the villager, ploughman, or whoever he was, was thinking of the increased grazing he could get for his cow if he stretched the boundaries a little? What he was losing on the common land he might regain on the roadsides. Though the ordinary rural resident of that time had very little education, he had an eye for the main chance, or a 'roard hoamwads'. Just an odd foot or two extra over a few miles could add considerably to the roadside grazing.

To get back to the Enclosures: Enclosure Commissioners varied from one to five in number; they were empowered to appoint one or two surveyors and with their aid the land was surveyed and valued. Priority was given to the tithe owner and Lord of the Manor (in this case, Sir Beaumont Hotham). In some cases the claim was settled by money payment, in one case £1.10.0 was paid for each oxgang (though not in this parish). Footpaths were also listed, though they are not shown on the 1771 map. It was estimated that 1,560 acres of East Yorkshire's 750,000 acres had been enclosed by 1717, but most of it took place at the latter part of the 18th century. On the Wolds it was rather later.

At this time, most of the land was assessed in oxgangs. The carucate in the Domesday Book was divided into eight oxgangs, so called because there were eight oxen in a normal plough team. Smaller teams were sometimes used so that areas of land varied greatly. In the Catwick Enclosures the oxgang worked out at roughly 15 acres.

Until the tractor came on the scene, farms were often described by the number of horses needed to work them. Thus a farm of 100 acres would be described as a 'fower hoss spot'. A farm on the Wolds of 700 or 800 acres would be described as a 'twenty hoss spot'. Of course, this depended on the type of land, but most agriculturalists could tell you the acreage of a farm by this description. So here we have a link with the past, though as the horses disappeared from the land and tractors took over, this centuries-old assessment went forever. I do not think anyone has got round to calculating the acreage of a farm by the number of tractors used.

In this parish there were 4,700 acres of land. 4,000 acres were divided among 40 people, most of them not from Hutton Cranswick.

Sir Beaumont Hotham	1,247 acres
R S Loyd	948 "
Rev M Mason	545 "
Rev M Sykes	345 "

Most of the land east of Skerne Road from Skerne Beck across to Scurf Dyke, and bordering Rotsea, went to Sir Beaumont Hotham, though as Lord of the Manor, the Hothams would have control of it in the first place. Sir Beaumont Hotham got one huge block of 559 acres; what is now Cranswick Grange land (once Hutton Common), and part of Corpslanding extending to Rotsea Bridge. The remainder went to Sykes, Loyd, Hudson and Mason; Robert Fox 21 acres and a Mr Keighley 53 acres.

The only road to the carrs went straight down Sheepman Lane and by Common Farm. Incidentally, the lands on both sides of Sheepman Lane are still very much in evidence, and like those in Corpslanding Road run from south to north.

On what is now the disused airfield, Rev. Mason got 72 acres for his 4 oxgangs and 1 cottage. On the south side of Southburn Road there were two blocks of land, 254 acres to R. S. Loyd and 244 acres to Sir Beaumont Hotham.

Here are a few interesting points from the Enclosures Map. Sir Beaumont Hotham got 130 acres for part of his great tithe and 19 acres for his small tithe. Great tithe was for the produce of arable land, wheat, oats etc.. Small tithe applied to livestock. Rev. M. Mason acquired 52 acres for tithe and 55 acres for glebe. Very few people in either Hutton or Cranswick owned their cottages, or the small fields and paddocks that went with them. Most of them belonged to Sir Beaumont Hotham. A smaller amount went to Rev. Dr Sykes and R. S. Loyd.

Here are most of those who owned a house and a small field or two in Hutton at the time of enclosure and would be classed as yeomen or freeholders, in fact typical villagers.

Ino Lambert had what was classed as an old enclosure in Beck Lane, Hutton. Next to it John Lambert with 5 acres. They may have been father and son. Ino Lambert also owned a house and a small paddock between Front Street (now Church Street) and Mill Street.

Thomas Barmby owned the cottage in Church Lane and a small field with it. This extended nearly up to the west of the church, and most of this was taken over for the churchyard extensions in 1909.

Robert Brown had 1 ½ acres near Hutton pit in Hutton Road.

Mrs Jane Walker possessed a cottage and small field at the bottom of Mill Street. This bordered the Hull to Driffield Road and was about 4 acres. She also had 9 acres at the bottom end of Jenkinson Lane (known locally as Jenky). The cottage where she lived has long since disappeared.

Richard Jenkinson owned a house and two paddocks in Jenkinson Lane (where Mr R Curtis now resides). They were a family of yeomen who were in this parish for over 100 years. Obviously this is where the lane gets its name.

In Cranswick those who owned a cottage and a small field attached were:

Isaac Stephenson : 3 acres in Hutton Road where the Council houses now stand.
W Wood : 4 acres at the bottom of Hutton Road.
Ino Taunton : 2 acres at the bottom of Hutton Road.

In Cranswick Main Street :
R Nickolson

Mary Sissons	J Stephenson
W Wood	W Usher
R Scaley	W Nickolson
M Dawson	John Coates

Mary Sissons also had a field of 2 acres in Heddlemere Lane, or Station Lane as it is now called.

In Southgate :
John Stephenson had a house and small paddock at the bottom of Southgate, as well as 20 acres about two or so miles away near Burn Butts, approximately where the market Weighton railway would run over 100 years later. John Stephenson was also classed as a yeoman farmer. 204 acres adjoining, now belonging to Burn Butts, was in the name of Robert Savage Loyd. Richardson Nicholson had 6 acres and a small field at the bottom of Cranswick village near Megginson Bridge. He also occupied a house and paddock behind the green near Jackey Garth. A Richard Nicholson is mentioned in the 1823 directory as a farmer. It may not have been the same man; if it was he must have been getting on in years, or it may have been his son. Nevertheless, it was the only name from the yeomen, freeholders, and cottagers of the Enclosures 50 years previously.

Mr Frank Nicholson, who often gave talks on local history in this district, has said that the field between Balk Lane and Jenkinson Lane were a perfect example of Enclosure. Bounded on the west by the Hull to Driffield road, and on the east by Mill Street, there will be approximately 50 acres. Some of it may have been enclosed before 1770. Centuries ago it was one large field between the four roads. It was 'landed up' in lands twelve to fourteen yards wide, and with the exception of two or three fields which have been cultivated and levelled, all the ridges are just as they were when ploughed up all those years ago.

If you ignore all the hedges you can visualise it as an open field growing corn. Those old furrows ('forrs') where the ploughman finished his work, 'scoored forr oot', seemed to last for ever when sown down to grass.

I remember one grassfield which had not been cultivated within living memory,. yet no measuring would be needed if it was ploughed again, as all the furrows left by some long dead ploughman stood square and true.

The old chalk pit near Chalk Pit cottages (on the 1856 map it is called Beladmont Pit) is not on the Enclosure map, so if the pit was opened after 1770 a tremendous amount of chalk must have been taken out in just over a hundred years. It belonged originally to Reynards of Sunderlandwick, until it was sold after the First World War. A man was regularly employed in the pit by the Sunderlandwick Estate. By the turn of the century it had been abandoned completely, left to grow into a miniature jungle, and became a children's playground. A popular pastime for the children of sixty odd years ago was to slide down the steep slopes on a piece of tin. If the ground was wet, so much the better; they could go faster. Needless to say, the tin and the rear end of the child often parted company and some of the children ended up in a sorry state.

The other pit in Hutton Road, now used as a council refuse tip, is marked on the Enclosure Map as the Stone Pit. It was the parish pit and may have been in existence for a very long time. The last chalk was taken out in 1930. It was then closed and used only as a refuse tip. It is now filled in and may revert to the parish as a sports field or playground. These old pits, which were often an embarrassment to the owners, and could hardly be given away, are now very much in demand for disposing of modern civilisation's rubbish.

A great many posts and rails were carried up the River Hull from the port of Hull to Corpslanding. From there they were distributed by wagon. During the eighteenth century many estate owners planted tree nurseries and, as these developed, the quickthorn hedges superseded the rail fences around the new enclosures. Sheep were a danger to the young hedges, and in some enclosure awards the Commissioners stipulated that livestock should be kept from the fields for ten years. Some of the old elms which predominate in this parish will have been planted about the time of enclosure. One which was cut down a few years ago, judging by its rings, had been planted in the latter part of the eighteenth century.

Many historians disagree about the injustice done to the ordinary villager or cottager who had held grazing rights on the common land since time immemorial, and injustice there must have been, though most of the awards of two to three acres were to those who held no land but a cottage, and could claim common rights now extinguished. It is said that the enclosures robbed the peasants of seven million acres of land. In many cases it took away their independence. He may have been in rags before, but at least he was more or less his own man. It used to be said before the Second World War that it was worth a pound a week to be your own boss, and a pound was a lot of money then!

It was comparatively easy for any person of power and influence to enclose common land. The Duke of Wellington was once encouraged by some of his associates to enclose some common land near his estate of Stratfield Saye in Hampshire. Wellington said he did not see why he should take over land which did not belong to him, and to which he had no claim.

Before we leave the subject of the Enclosures, one old village family, the Fox family, is worthy of mention. They were described as yeomen farmers in the seventeenth and eighteenth century parish records. At the time of the Enclosures, Robert Fox had seven acres of land on the Hull to Driffield road. Fisher's plant is built on part of it. This field is known locally as Tommy Krobs. He also owned the house where R Welbourne carried on his tailoring business for many years. This is nearly opposite the telephone kiosk in Cranswick Main Street. The row of tiny cottages next to the Pack Horse public house and the farm of Swinekeld were in his name, with 21 acres in Sheepman Lane, near where Little Common Farm now stands. His land amounted to just over 30 acres. This included a little paddock on Hobman Lane of 2 acres. His stock would graze on the green and the roadside verges along with other villagers' animals in charge of a 'cow tenter'.

There is a tombstone, laid flat, on the north side of Hutton Church, near the water tap; on it is inscribed:

> Robt. Fox 24 years of age died Dec 1778, also his son Robt who died 1779 aged 11 years and Margaret, wife of Robt. Fox who died Oct 1819.

Could this have been the Robt. Fox whose name is on the Enclosure Map? If so, he must have been very young, or there may have been father and son of the same name. The son aged 11 could hardly have been his natural son. After nearly 200 years the name disappeared when Ellen Fox died at Hutton in 1847. Though the name has gone, there may still be their descendants living in the village today.

CHAPTER SEVEN

THE TURNPIKE TRUSTS

Thousands of feet have trod these roads and lanes, Saxons, Normans, villeins and thanes.
Soldier returning from the wars again,
With the sailor from some far flung foreign main.

Turnpike Trusts were set up in the eighteenth century, and these empowered private individuals to make stretches of road, keep them in good condition, and levy tolls to finance these projects. So the toll bars and toll houses were set up in suitable places. These were usually in a narrow part of a road, or near a stream where there was no other way round, such as the one near Bar Bridge, Sunderlandwick.

Previous to this the roads were in a shocking state. Some of them were practically impassable in winter, and in rainy weather. Many people in the country were marooned for most of the winter months, especially those who had no river or waterway nearby.

So the Turnpike Trusts commenced operations, and the surveyors could take furze, heath, stones, gravel or sand from common or waste ground, river or brook, without paying. Trustees could build one or more gates across the road, and also erect a toll house at or near each gate. Here are some examples of the tolls levied (these are from White Cross, Leven to Norwood in Beverley):

For every chariot, landau, chaise, chair or hearse drawn by six horses or mules	1 s.	6d.
For every wagon, cart, or carriage; The felloes of the wheels being nine inches Wide, drawn by five draught animals	1s.	0d.
A Wagon drawn by one		4d.
For every horse of more unladen		1 ½d.
Calves or sheep per score		5d.

The toll collector was empowered to take what assistance he required to distrain any horse, cattle or carriage with load in payment of any toll due.

These tolls were to be paid once a day, and all disputes were to be settled by a Justice of the Peace. Anyone carrying material for road repairs, dung, lime or compost for manuring land in the township, hay, straw and corn were exempt, also implements of husbandry such as ploughs and harrows and people going to and from church and chapel. Clergymen going upon their ministerial duties, soldiers on the march and vagrants sent by legal passes were exempt.

Any person trying to evade paying tolls, such as going round the side of the toll bar, or permitting people to go over lands to unload goods, had to forfeit the sum of forty shillings for each offence.

On 1 May 1766 a meeting was held at the Tiger Inn in Beverley, when it was decided that another turnpike gate be erected between the new bridge and the road leading to Sunderlandwick. (In the Parish Register the vicar records that the Beverley to Driffield turnpike was set up at Poundsworth Hook (this was the same place) on Whit Monday afternoon 1766).

A Christopher Cooper of Lund was to be the toll collector. A toll collector had an allowance made to him out of the tolls of twenty shillings a year. He was also paid five shillings a week. On 18 August 1878 the Turnpike Trust decided that Richard Porter should build the Sunderlandwick toll house. This old house, Bar House, as it was always known, was demolished in 1969. Whether there was a house there in the years between 1766 and 1787 we do not know. Maybe the poor old toll collector had to live in some kind of temporary shack for these twenty - one years.

On 23 June 1787 the Clerk to the Trust was instructed to write to T Baxter of Bell Mills telling him that if he allowed any person to pass through his grounds to avoid paying tolls, both he and the person passing through it would be prosecuted. Two months later the Trust requested that T Baxter be asked to lock up the gate on the new bridge near his mill, and to indict any person who broke it down.

I have heard my father say that travellers from Hutton to Driffield often went round by Skerne to avoid the toll bar at Sunderlandwick. So the bridge at Bell Mills must have been a sore point with the Trust, judging by the way it came down on the master of Bell Mills. In spite of all the Trust's vigilance, there must have been many ways though the fields where the locals especially could have dodged the tolls.

The toll bars and houses were never popular, and they were sometimes attacked by mobs and set on fire. The odd one or two left in the country today are also not very popular, and apparently there will be another if the Humber Bridge is ever finished.

There seems to be no record of the toll bar house which stood at the bottom of South Hall Hill, Cranswick, and was pulled down a few years ago. In his book Piety among the Peasantry (1889), J H Woodcock tells of a Methodist minister whose horse 'galloped away' with him on the

Driffield to Beverley high road. The Cranswick toll gates were wide open and the minister and his fiery steed went straight through. John Dixon was the toll barkeeper in 1851. He was also a blacksmith and his services would often be required when the roads were slippery in winter. The horses would require 'sharping' as it was called. This meant putting frost studs in their shoes to keep the animals on their feet in frosty weather.

At the time the Turnpike Trusts commenced operations, the stage coaches were coming into being. Indeed, it is said that the first one appeared in Yorkshire in the reign of Charles the Second, so better roads were needed as the coaches ran between all the principal towns.

According to Baines directory of 1823, the Wellington coach went to Bridlington and Scarborough every morning in summer, and three days a week in winter at 10.00 am from Driffield. Another one left for Hull at 11.45 am. However, there was a coach with the name of the 'British Queen' running between Hull and Scarborough, and it was probably the one going to Hull. It would arrive at Cranswick at about 12 o'clock, depending on the weather, and call at the Decoy Inn, Dennison's Arms, Londesborough Arms or New Inn, as the hostelry opposite Burn Butts Road end has been known over the years. There it would pick up any passengers and leave the post.

At this time, before Rowland Hill's penny post of 1840, a letter from any post office in England going no further than 15 measured miles cost 4d; above fifteen and not exceeding twenty miles, 5d; above twenty and not over thirty, 6d. There are other rates gradually increasing until we get to: above two hundred and thirty miles and not over three hundred, one shilling. However, as many of the population at that time could not write their names, the price of letters would not affect the ordinary individual very much. At the present time, over 150 years later, with all the advantages of modern transport, we seem to be moving towards a situation of dear postage again. So much for progress.

The coming of the railways heralded the end of the stage coach. The roads also came under the jurisdiction of the local authority, and the old Turnpike Trusts are now relics of the past. The railways have also passed their heyday, and traffic (with the internal combustion engine) is back on the roads again. So we seem to have gone full circle.

CHAPTER EIGHT

CONDITIONS AT THE END OF THE EIGHTEENTH CENTURY

After the Enclosures the state of the villager was often worse than before. Many of them had lost their bit of land, and the commons where they could graze their stock. Some went into the towns, and those who stayed had their wages subsidised through the Poor Rate.

Typical wages at that time were:-

12s. a week and small beer
7s a week in winter
Reaping 6s. 6d. To 7s. 9d. an acre
Mowing grass on the Wolds: 1s. and 9d: 4s. 6d. on the lowlands
Hoeing turnips: 5s. 6d. per acre
Threshing wheat: 2s. 6d. per quarter
Barley and peas: 1s. 0d per quarter
Oats: 9d. per quarter

(Turnips were just becoming popular in the East Riding. A quarter of wheat was 36 stones; one of oats was 24; one of barley was 32.)

There were two sacks to every quarter and so it remained until the 1920's when all corn was sold by the hundredweight and 16 stone was the maximum weight in a bag. At this period of the eighteenth century the corn was threshed by the flail, as threshing machines belonged to the next century.

Wages for all kinds of farming servants were £12 a year
Ploughlads £ 7 a year
Dairywomen £ 5 a year

These would be hired by the year and living in.

Cost of provisions:-

Beef 3d. per lb
Mutton 3d. per lb
Butter 5 ½d per lb
Labourers' house rents 20s. per year
Poor Rates 6d. in the pound

Farmers complained about the high price of labour. There were so many public works going on, such as draining, Enclosure and making turnpikes, that there was great competition for labour. As the Napoleonic Wars were approaching, the Army also took many men.

All in all, the countryside was a bit more prosperous, as corn prices were quite good with the imminence of war, though it is doubtful whether any of this prosperity filtered through to the ordinary villager or farm worker. The town workers were still in a minority, but the gap was closing fast, and the Industrial Revolution was approaching.

The age of steam was just around the corner, and this was to lighten the labours of the country man. Jethro Tull had invented the corn drill, and Viscount Townshend had popularised the growing of the turnip, which meant more stock could be kept through the winter. By the 1960's the turnip had nearly disappeared from the fields of East Yorkshire but now, due to the increased cost of feed, is coming back once more, but it is not grown on the scale it used to be.

CHAPTER NINE

THE NAPOLEONIC WARS

There is no record of the people of this parish being directly concerned with anti-invasion plans, but they must have been very much involved. In the last years of the eighteenth century plans were made to evacuate all the people living in the coastal regions of Holderness and move them westwards. Wagons were kept ready in some of the villages, and priority was given to the aged and the sick. If there was an enemy landing, all stocks of grain and food near the coast, which could not be taken inland, had to be destroyed. This, in the Second World War, was practised effectively by the Russians and was called a 'scorched earth' policy. The roads of Holderness at the end of the eighteenth century were in such a bad state that most of the food-stuffs would have had to be left behind and destroyed.

The Government was getting worried about grain supplies as the French wars kept dragging on. Food prices had risen and this had caused disaffection among the civilian population. Morale was also low in the Navy. In the late summer of 1801 the Home Office sent out forms to the ministers of every parish. They had to visit all the farmers and obtain details of all crops. The form for Hutton Cranswick parish is not dated, but like all the others would have been sent out just before the harvest. The curate in charge of this parish was the Rev. John Stanley and he had to visit all the farmers and find out what were the crop prospects for the coming harvest. He was not a professional valuer and would have to rely on what the farmers told him. No doubt he got some queer answers.

Some farmers, as still happens today, would tell him that their 'turnout' (yield) would be far higher than it could possibly be. Others would say very little. Some would be just plain 'orkerd'. In South Yorkshire one of the vicars called public meetings and spent several days trying to get information to compile an accurate record. The Rev. John Stanley just gave the figures for this parish and does not state whether the farmers co-operated or not.

Wheat, 950 acres
It is thought that wheat will produce three quarters an acre, Winchester measure, upon an average which in this parish is a very good crop.
Barley, 132 acres
Oats, 536 acres

Barley and oats expected to produce five quarters an acre.
Potatoes   14 acres
Very few potatoes are grown, but this crop is tolerable.
Peas and Beans   423 acres
Peas and beans a tolerable crop
Turnips   55 acres
Very good
Maslin   19 acres

(John Stanley)

Wheat at three quarters an acre (1 ton, 1 cwt) does not seem very good by present-day standards when often double that quantity is produced. It may be considered quite good when we take into account the fact that a lot of this land where John Stanley recorded the farmers' assessment of the wheat crop was, just before the Second World War, producing about the same. The barley and oats at five quarters was good, as most of this land was, and still is, more suitable for wheat.

The 14 acres of potatoes would be grown by the farmers in small lots for their own consumption. The peas and beans described, like the potatoes, as a tolerable crop, we today should call just 'middling'. The beans would be ploughed in at the 'back end', Autumn, and no doubt they would be sown as they were in the early part of this century, every 'thod forr' (third furrow). By this method they could be hoed between the rows. The peas were what they called grey peas, though they were more brown than grey. These were the type used for making 'carlins', when they were boiled, fried in fat and eaten at Easter. Both the peas and beans could be fed to stock whole. If they were 'steeped' (soaked) until they were soft they could be fed to most adult stock.

Turnips were then somewhat of an unknown quantity and East Yorkshire farmers were slow to adopt this crop. The farmers of Hutton Cranswick parish may have found out that clay land does not always grow good turnips.

'Maslin' was a crop of mixed corn, usually barley and oats sown together. It seems to have been a popular crop in the eighteenth century. During the Second World War, the Government encouraged farmers to sow a mixture of oats, barley and peas. The idea was alright, but there was often trouble harvesting this kind of crop as the oats and barley were often ripe and the peas green. This crop was grown for stock feeding as the peas supplied valuable protein.z

The Rev. John Stanley's record tells us nothing of the hay crop of this parish, neither does it state the acreage of grass or the amount of corn which the animals could be expected to consume.

After the Battle of Trafalgar on 21 October 1805, the invasion precautions were relaxed. The French Navy had taken such a battering that it was in no fit state to promote an invasion. There was a slight scare when Napoleon escaped from Elba, but after Waterloo in 1815 there were no further invasion threats in the East Riding until Hitler in 1940.

CHAPTER TEN

THE EARLY NINETEENTH CENTURY

Hutton Cranswick in 1823, from Baines Directory

At that time the population of the parish was 917. Twelve years previously it was 748. At this time, 1823, the population of Hornsea was only 790, Driffield 2,303, Bridlington 4,275, Watton 307, and Skerne 251. The population of the seaside resorts has increased tremendously since then.

Here are the tradesmen and farmers listed in the above Directory. They may be only a cross section of those in the village or parish.

Blacksmiths:
William Bowers and John Norriss (Bowers could have been a mistake and maybe should have been Bowes, as the Bowes family were blacksmiths in the nineteenth century).

Farmers:
George Baulby
John Carlton (this maybe should have been Catton, as John Catton was farming South Hall in the early years of the nineteenth century).
Thomas Cole
Matthew Danby
Thomas Denton
William Dawson
John Fletcher (Hutton)
William Goodlass
Robert Granger
Joseph Granger
Richard Nicholson
David Pinder
John Simpson
James Wilkinson
Andrew Williamson

Joiners:
Thomas Newlove
Francis Summerson

Public Houses:
Pack Horse, Thomas Barmby
Decoy Inn, William Bilton
Board Inn, William Forth
Board Inn, William Goodlass (Hutton)

Schoolmasters:
Richard Vaukes
Robert Richardson, schoolmaster at the old school at the bottom of Hutton Road and also a shopkeeper.

Shoemakers:
George Brown
Christopher Hessey
Antony Parker

Shopkeepers:
Robert Dove
Francis Jennison
Robert Richardson
Margaret Stephenson

Tailors:
John Sanderson
George Sanderson
Mark Todd

Wheelwrights:
W Anderson
J Wilson

Ropemaker:
William Best

Corn Miller:
Thomas Dawson (Hutton) also Poundsworth and Riverhead, Driffield.

Carriers:
John Booth
George Summerson

CHAPTER ELEVEN

EARLY VICTORIAN DAYS

Now we move on to 1840, though this list from White's Directory has been slightly abbreviated.

Hutton:
Public Houses:
Board Inn, W Goodlass
Beer Houses:
John Ashley
W Garton
Blacksmith:
T Martindale
Corn Millers:
T Dawson
Moses Hayton

Cranswick:
Inns and Taverns:
Cross Keys, R Gowthorpe
Denisons Arms, John Vernon
Pack Horse, Mary Barmby
Beer Houses:
R Goodlass
W Walker
Blacksmiths:
J Allison
W Bowes
R Ramsdale
Boot and Shoemakers:
W Barker
J Brown
R Spink
D Turner
J Wilson
Farmers:
J Caton (South Hall)
J Dunn
G Dobson
J Kirby
J Granger
Schoolmasters:
F Jennison
F Riley

Farmers:
J Boyes
J Dalby (Corpslanding)
W Goodlass
A Parker
W Waite
J Wilkinson
Shopkeepers:
J Massinder
F Riley
Methodist Minister:
R Kirby

Shopkeepers:
R Dove
R Gowthorpe
J Jameson
R Macdonald
Tailors:
J Hodgson
E Sanderson
John Sanderson
Geo Sanderson
Carriers:
T Ellis
Mary Summerson
J Cook
Ropemaker:
W Kelsey
Butchers:
John Barmby
W Lowe

35

At this time the young Queen Victoria had just commenced her long reign. This first period of her life has always been known as the 'hungry forties'. This was attributed to the Corn Laws, which caused corn to reach a higher price and brought much misery to the poorer classes. In 1846 the corn duty was lowered, and later was abolished altogether.

The worker in the fields was receiving 7s. a week and the threshing machine was in use in the East Riding. A Miles Smith, who farmed Sunderlandwick, was using one in 1812, though it was said to have run too slow, did not make a very good job, and was left to rot. There were a few teething troubles, but these machines had come to stay, and they put an end to the laborious practice of threshing with the flail. They rendered good service until superseded by the combine. Ransomes, Fosters, Clayton and Shuttleworth, and Marshalls were all successful makers of threshing machines and steam engines. The early machines were horse driven, and four or six horses went round and round turning a shaft which was something like a universal joint. This was known as a 'hoss pairt'.

The same sort of thing was used to drive barn machinery, such as a choppy cutter where the shaft went through the barn wall, and the horse went round and round outside. There were sometimes one or two lying about on farms forty or fifty years ago, though these had long since turned for the last time. If any could be found in reasonable working order, they are now valuable as collectors' items. One of these driven by a horse was used for pumping water until 1925 at Burn Butts. Then it was replaced with a petrol engine.

These new-fangled threshing machines were not received very favourably by some of the farm workers, who could see an end to the winter flail threshing. In some parts of the country they were broken up by mobs, and sometimes set on fire. In the 1830's there were cases of stack burning and machine breaking in Lincolnshire and the East and West Ridings of Yorkshire. At York the Magistrates warned the inhabitants of the severe penalties which could be imposed. Most of the machine breaking occurred in the South of England. Some of those who were brought before the courts were sentenced to transportation.

Much the same thing happened in this present century as the combine replaced the threshing machine and put an end to 'tramp threshing', as it was known then ('tramp threshing' meant following the machine round the parish all the winter, and it usually meant more or less regular employment until the spring came round again), though there was no opposition or violence. Most of the workers had come to realise that machinery could be a great boon.

CHAPTER TWELVE

LIFE IN THE MIDDLE OF THE NINETEENTH CENTURY

None of the persons mentioned in this chapter is a fictional character. They are actual people who lived in this parish all those years ago when life was hard and rough. They served their day and generation to the best of their ability, and got very little recompense. Every generation thinks it has been born too soon, and this one could have real justification for thinking so. Those of us now enjoying the benefits of the Welfare State, who can look back across the years and make comparisons, will understand the conditions they endured. Though on second thoughts, can we understand them, being so cushioned from adversity.

In this chapter I will try to describe the parish of Hutton Cranswick and how the people lived from the 1840's into the 1860's, much of it based on the 1851 census. At this time the agricultural worker would be getting 7s. a week (thirty years later he was only getting 10s.), and even though at that time beef was only 7s. or 8s. a stone and a village then was practically self supporting, a few shillings would only stretch so far. Most of the inhabitants would only scrape a mere existence, the self-employed tradesmen included.

The farm worker, like the ploughman in Gray's Elegy, still plodded his way homewards on the footpaths through the fields. Winter and summer he would be expected to be at work by 6.00 am, which for some of them meant leaving home at 5.00 am (though in winter the hours had to be shortened due to the failing light). Leaving work at 6.00 pm he might get home about 7.00 pm. The rest of the day or night was his own. Good old days they are sometimes called by people who should know better. Needless to say, there were no holidays.

Now the Ramblers Association always seem to be having legal battles with all and sundry over these old paths. Where the villagers on their way to work struggled across a plank over a stream in the dark, the ramblers (who sometimes only use these paths two or three times a year) are now provided with elaborate and costly bridges at the ratepayers' expense.

The population of this parish in 1851 was 1,276. The census at this time gives the ages of the inhabitants of this parish from a month old baby to the 97 year old mother of Richard Peck, a pauper.

Some of the infants recorded as two or three year olds I can remember as old men. The families were not unduly large, about seven was the largest, and there were many of only two or three. The families seemed to be larger in the early part of the next century, though the population did not increase much.

Taking the period 5 October 1850 to 5 October 1851 there were 23 burials. Of these seven were just recorded as infants, another three were under four years of age.

To move on to 1857, there were 38 deaths that year and 40 baptisms. There were seven consecutive deaths of infants from 1 September to 16 October. The next to follow them into the churchyard was William Kelsey, aged 93. He was a member of the family of ropers who lived near Station Lane, Cranswick. These seven children who died in little over a month must have been the victims of an epidemic. Those who survived their childhood years became more or less immune to germs and, like William Kelsey, often lived far beyond their allotted span. Earlier during that year another four infants died, as well as a child of four, another five and a twelve year old girl. The number of baptisms (forty) for 1857 was rather higher than usual; about twenty - five was the norm. That was the pattern through most of the nineteenth century. By the end of it the deaths of the very young were getting fewer. In 1900 the infant mortality rate (those under one year old) over the whole country was 154 per 1,000. In 1967 it was 18.3.

At this time, doctoring, or curing ailments of any kind, seemed to be a do it yourself job. Most villages possessed a woman who attended confinements, laid out those who had passed on, lanced boils (botches, as they used to be called), and dosed their patients with home made medicines. Such a one was Mary Petch, who lived in the house next door to the fish shop in the Main Street, along with her husband and daughter Susannah, assistant teacher at the Infant School. Mary Petch was the village doctor for fifty years, and was said to be a wonderful healer. She also brought up nine children, was a staunch Methodist, and lived to be nearly ninety. She tried to heal their souls as well as their bodies.

There was also an old lady at Skerne who performed the same kind of service, and after Mary Petch passed on people from this village often walked to Skerne for treatment.

These healers of the poor were usually well-respected members of a village community with a wonderful sense of service, though if anybody had said that to them they would have been the first to disagree.

Some of the vets also possessed no academic qualifications. There is no record of them venturing into the field of human medicine, unlike the vets in the Wild West films who treated humans and animals alike with careless abandon, though I can remember one man from Cranswick dosing his young daughter with some medicine which the vet had given him for a calf. This vet, or farrier as they were often called, was unqualified. The girl was suffering from some mysterious disease, and according to the father was completely cured.

Now we will take a look at the people and their way of life somewhere about a century and a quarter ago. It is difficult to say exactly where some of them resided, but the public houses, the farms, and some of the shops can be located. From this we can find roughly where most of the people lived, and where some of them worked, although some of the houses, most of them thatched cottages, have gone. For instance, there was a row of cottages where the Foresters' Hall now stands. Scraps of information handed down from previous generations are also invaluable.

At this time Lord John Russell was Liberal Prime Minister. The Duke of Wellington was in the last full year of his life (he died in 1852) and the Crimean War was only three years away.

The repeal of the Corn Laws was supposed to usher in a period of prosperity, though I do not suppose the ordinary tradesman, farmworker, or other villager noticed much difference.

Oxen were used as draught animals in East Yorkshire until about 1845. If the horses got stuck with a load they were often taken out, and oxen yoked up to pull the wagon out. Though better pullers, the oxen were too slow, and were ousted by the horses; they in the next century being superseded by the tractor. In his Peninsular campaign Wellington preferred oxen, as they could live on rough grass and most kinds of roughage, where a horse would starve. Bullocks like long grass, whilst a horse prefers it short and sweet. Anyone who has worked among stock will know that a bullock or cow is far hardier, and can stand illness and rough conditions better than a horse. Where a horse with colic or 'gripes' as it is often called, is soon rolling about on the floor, a bullock is usually determined to 'grin and bear it'.

Like most villages in East Yorkshire (and unlike many in the West Riding), the Industrial Revolution passed through this one. The railway came in 1846 and the stage coach soon disappeared from the roads forever. The track where the carts took chalk from Hutton pit across the fields to build the rail track can still be traced. The railways brought the towns nearer to the villages and in many ways revolutionised travel. Though it could hardly be described as luxurious, it was much faster than the old stage coaches.

The Hull to Bridlington railway was officially opened on 6 October 1846, and when the train of sixty-six carriages, drawn by three engines, Antelope, Aerial and Hudson, left Hull it was a wet day. By the time the train had reached Cottingham the weather was a great deal better, which made it more pleasant for the crowds along the route. It seems that

Beverley did not join in the rejoicing, as they had a celebration on 31 July when the Directors made an official survey of the railroad, and the workmen had a feast of cheese, bread and ale with the Beverley Iron Works Brass Band in attendance.

When the train reached Driffield it too joined in the festivities, though there had been opposition in the town, possibly from those connected with the canal, who could foresee a loss of trade. Then to Bridlington where there was a procession round the town, and a luncheon in the station goods yard shed, with the celebrations ending in Hull that same evening. The Hull to Bridlington line was originally meant to be a single one, but the contractors, Jackson and Bean, installed a double track and electric telegraph. The engineer was J. C. Birkenshaw of York.

Those early trains were very primitive, and the driver simply stood on a platform behind the engine. The passengers were just as much exposed and in the early days third class was often an open wagon, sometimes without seats. The travellers must have got as black as sweeps. The aristocracy took a dim view of rail travel at first, and preferred the stage coach, though it was all right for their servants. Perhaps they did not like being too near the 'great unwashed'. Then the railways placed a coach body on an open wagon. The Duke of Wellington used this means of travel until his death.

The railways, like the canals in the preceding century, attracted all kinds of roughnecks and itinerant workers during their construction. There was good money to be made, and nobody bothered much about safety or any other regulations. When the Market Weighton line was built about forty five years after the Hull to Bridlington one, an amorous railway builder was castrated by a group of the local husbands.

George Hudson, the Railway King, built the Hull to Bridlington railway. Hudson was no ordinary man. Born at Howsham, between Malton and York in 1800, he started work in a drapers shop in York. Having been left a considerable amount of money by his father, he started building railways all over England, and said he would bring them all to York. In 1849 his companies collapsed because they couldn't pay their dividends, and Hudson was disgraced. He died in London in obscurity in 1871. George Hudson may have had more than a fleeting connection with this parish, as White's Directory of 1840 in a note on the church states:

> Two sums of 51s. each from Mason and Barkers' charged on the rectorial tithes of Hutton Cranswick and now in the impropriation of George Hudson Esq. Of York.

This must have been the Railway King himself.

Cranswick was said to have been a rough kind of place in the middle years of the last century, although I suppose it was no worse than many other villages of that period. Hutton is not mentioned, only Cranswick in that respect, so they must have all been respectable citizens at Hutton, even though it possessed a public house and at one time two beer houses.

Before the Methodists got their own two chapels built, they used to hold meetings in all kinds of places - barns or anything with a roof. G. Bullock, a respected local preacher, once preached in a place where there were, amongst other things, seventy stolen hams hidden. Of course, this was no reflection on the worshippers. These must have been some of the hams which made Cranswick notorious, because in the early days of the railroad, when a train stopped in the station, some of the passengers would stick their heads out and shout 'Hutton for mutton and Cranswick for bacon'.

Some of the locals used to wait for the trains coming in and there were often fights. One man was going to shout 'Hutton for mutton and Cranswick for bacon, but when he got to 'ba...' somebody gave him a hefty clout in the mouth. The police were called and in time it all died down. Though where the 'Hutton for mutton' came in, nobody seems to know. Years later, if anybody said they came from either of the two villages somebody was sure to mention the mutton and bacon. Some of the bacon was said to have been hidden down the well on the green, long since filled in. According to another old tale, there was then only one honest man in Cranswick and he stole a saddle. Whatever the merits of that one, the bacon episode is quite true.

At this time there would be eight or ten horses of different sizes on the green. They belonged to the carriers, coalmen, tradesmen and others, some of whom possessed a bit of land. Sometimes there would be the odd mule or donkey. They were all workhorses, had to earn a living, and help their owners to earn one too. There were no fancy riding horses; everything was strictly utilitarian.

The Driffield Times of 1860 cost 1d, and in the first year of its life tells us that wheat on the London Corn Exchange was 42s. to 52s. per quarter (a quarter was 36 stones). A sheep stealer got four years' penal servitude, and R Tate of Driffield sold washing machines from £2 to £6. Holloway's ointment was advertised as a panacea for all ills, including bad legs, cocobay, yaws, cancer and about twenty other diseases. W. Scruton was charged at court with neglecting his business by Mr Spink, blacksmith of Cranswick. The defence was that he was ill and, not being able to pay expenses (7s. 6d.) his father would not do so - he was committed to durance vile'.

Corn Cutting was 7s. an acre; that would be cutting with the scythe, or ley' as it is still called in East Yorkshire. That must have been quite a decent wage, though it does not say what kind of corn it was. So much could depend on whether it was a good standing crop or one that was laid. A good standing crop of barley would be much easier to deal with than a laid crop of wheat. It was often said that a good mower could cut an acre a day, though this was the exception rather than the rule. It takes years to become adept with a scythe, though it looks just a bull-headed job, and a casual onlooker might think it was fit only for someone weak in the head and strong in the back or arms.

To get a razor-like edge on a scythe was the first essential. If a sixpence could be stuck on the edge of a blade it was said to be sharp. However much a craftsman the man with the 'ley' may have been, under a hot August sun is was sheer hard graft. I remember one man, born about 1860, whose father told him about a foreman who was leading a gang of mowers on a farm on the edge of this parish, when the master came over and said 'Scale 'em Caleb' (he meant 'Go Faster; leave the others behind'. Then they would have to work faster to keep up. The farmer used to prime Caleb with beer on the side. It was surprising how much work was done for a pint of beer in those days. When most of the corn had to be carried off the wagons into the Riverhead corn depots at Driffield, there was usually somebody hanging about who would carry a lot of corn for the price of a pint.

Most of the tradesmen in the villages at that time hired for a month at harvest. Even when the corn had been cut it was all to gather up, tie up and stook. Children were often pressed into service to 'mak bands' for typing up the sheaves. All this needed a considerable amount of labour, as there were so many processes to go through before the corn even got into the stack, but labour was cheap, overtime was non-existent, and a six day week persisted until the Forst World War.

Cutting corn with a scythe seemed to linger on even after the flail had been consigned to the scrap heap, and the threshing machine was in general use. The first reaper in this district was the Crosskill, which was pushed on the front of three horses, and just dropped the corn in a swathe at the side. This type of machine was invented in 1826 by Patrick Bell, a young Divinity student. It was little used for the next twenty-five years, but at the Great Exhibition at Crystal Palace in 1851, three machines were on show, Bell's and two others from America. From then on these reapers became more popular. The driver walked behind and acted as a kind of steersman, as there was a pole, something like a wagon pole with a weight on the end, between two of the horses. The drivers liked to see how straight they could lay the 'swearthes' (swathes), and I remember my father telling me how he was once sent up the road by the farmer to look at a field he had just cut in order to admire his handiwork.

Steering the machine was hard work, and often meant a 'wet shet' (shirt), but at least it was then a great improvement on the scythe. Crosskills was the old Beverley firm then it its heyday. Not so long ago there were old iron-tyred carts in this district with the name of Crosskill. They also patented a big steam-driven rotavator.

Then came the put-off, which needed two men, one to drive the two horses, and the other to manipulate a rake and a platform made of lathes to make the 'shavs' (sheaves). The rake was used to pull the corn onto the platform after the knife had cut it. The lathe platform was worked by a foot lever, and when a sheaf was collected it was dropped. This could be hard work in certain crops, but this was an advancement, as the corn did not need to be pulled into sheaves with the gathering rake. These machines were simply grass reapers which could be converted to corn cutting, a kind of dual purpose machine. The Bamford grass reapers of the 1920's were still being turned out with attachments for fitting an extra seat and a set of lathes for collecting the corn.

I had one of these old Bamford reapers and all the fittings from an old put-off which had not been used since before the First World War until quite recently, when they went for scrap and firewood. This could have been assembled to make a perfect working machine from the late century, providing you could find a pair of horses to yoke to it (a tractor would seem out of place). There may be some of these old reapers in some museum or collection of vintage machinery, though I have never seen one. So another link with the past disappears.

The last of these non-tying reapers was the Samuelson sail reaper, fitted with six large sails which swept the corn off at intervals in a sheaf ready for tying up. The sails were geared in such a way that when they looked as if they were going to clout the driver over the head they suddenly shot up in the air and came down again. The old sail reapers were used after the selfbinder came into use, as it was often said that corn cut and tied up straight away would never get ready for stacking. Many farmers thought the corn should be loose for a while and dry out before being tied up. Maybe a few wet harvests made them think otherwise. Needless to say, all these machines are very much collectors' items, and are worth more than when they were new all those years ago.

At that time, and for a long while after, everything was geared to agriculture, and the community was practically self-supporting. The village tailor made the suits (mass production of clothing was in the far distant future), and the cobbler made the boots. Everyone baked their own bread. What could not be obtained from the various travelling salesmen and pedlars was stocked in Driffield. Even when the railway came, many people, often whole families, still walked there and back until the First World War when bicycles became popular. A shopping trip to Driffield was a red letter day as they were few and far between.

The inhabitants of the village and parish in 1851   (from the Census)

> The enumerator did his survey in sections. Here is one of them: Part of the parish of Hutton Cranswick, comprising the north side of the Main Street from John Hodgson's tailor shop to the bottom of the town. The whole of the south side of the street with the Green, Southgate, Gannock or Ganwick Farm. The Decoy Inn, Denisons Arms, Goodlasses, The Turnpike Gatehouse, and Cattons Farm, Southall.

For obvious reasons we can only pick out names of most interest, especially those who were here long before there was any census, or those whose jobs and trades are of particular interest, and names of places still familiar. The number of paupers can also give us an insight into the living conditions.

Starting from somewhere at the top end of the Green was John Jameson, grocer and farmer of three acres. Most of the tradesmen of that time owned or rented a bit of land. Next was an empty house. There were quite a few empty houses in the village, though none was recorded elsewhere in the parish. There were several deserted wives in the village, and there was one with a family of three on parish relief next door to what is now the White Horse public house. Then, it was just a beerhouse occupied by Henry Watson, bricklayer and beer house keeper. He had family of five, and one of these was Charles who later built the school in 1875, and ended his days at Jubilee Farm, Hutton.

Opposite the pond was Robert Ramsdale, blacksmith. Then there was a quick succession of tradesmen; Christopher Sissons, carpenter; Bethel Wilkinson, cordwainer and a native of the village; Thomas Sissons, joiner and wheelwright, also a native; Francis Summerson, wheelwright, another old village family. William Lovell, butcher, was at the premises occupied by Mr W Atkinson until Spring 1979, when he retired. Adjoining were Robert Love, grocer, and Richard Bielby, cordwainer or shoemaker. There was also a man described as a 'vendor of oils', though what kind of oils he purveyed we are not told.

In Robin Hood Row lived Sara Morriss, a deserted wife and

charwoman, with a family of four all under eight. She was not on parish relief, so she must have managed to keep herself and children on her earnings. (Living nearly one hundred years before the Welfare State, women such as these must have had a miserable existence.) Her next door neighbour, Mary Evans, unmarried and with two children, was in a similar situation. She took in a family of four as lodgers, and the few shillings a week she got from them would help to eke out her meagre earnings. We who live in the latter part of the twentieth century may wonder how these people managed to exist; so may the people of a century and a quarter onwards think the same about us. On the other hand they may envy us.

The premises now occupied by Mr Frank Brown were then the Robin Hood public house. Joseph Barmby, 27 and Cranswick born, was the licensee. He was also a tailor and had a niece of fourteen employed as a servant, a nephew of sixteen as a tailor's apprentice, and a chimney sweep as a lodger. Before the end of the century the old pub lost its licence.

At the Pack Horse public house was a man named Robson. He was classified as an innkeeper, butcher and farmer of thirteen acres. Next to Heddlemere Lane, or Station Lane, lived William Kelsey, roper. He was a widower, and with him as son-in-law Robert Weatherill, with his wife Maria (Cranswick born) and their son, John, of ten months. They also had a kitchen maid of thirteen years and an errand boy of twelve. These two would live in and be paid by the year, probably not much for then, £5 or £6. Most children at that time left school at twelve, some even earlier. Compulsory schooling was nearly a quarter of a century away, and these children were expected to work any hours the employer wished.

The station and railway were now five years old, and the station master was William Taylor. At the bottom of Cranswick was East Vale, now known as Westfield: 166 acres and farmed by Robert Kirby, who employed two labourers. Now we come to what was called Green End, which may have meant the back of the green. Here were Samuel Sanderson, 53, a freeholder, occupying 10 acres, with his brother Johnson Sanderson, 56, free holder. These two were rough diamonds and made quite a bit of money by cattle dealing, and were not above a bit of sharp practice. 'Auld Sammy', as he was commonly known, owned a considerable amount of property in Hutton. They both turned over a new leaf and became pillars of the Methodist church. During a sermon, if it was too long, Johnson shouted 'Amen' twice; if it grew very long he gave three 'Amens' in quick succession. The preacher then knew it was time to stop. Both lived to a ripe old age. Sammy died in 1880 aged 83 and Johnson was 79 when he died in 1873.

Next to them were three uninhabited houses, and Henry Nicholson, a tea dealer. There seemed to be a tea dealer in most villages. Mary Summerson of Greenside was one of the village carriers, aided by her son. In the Directory of 1840 she was listed as a carrier, and in 1821 G Summerson was also a carrier.

The primary school now stands on what used to be Rat Row. There was nothing of note, except that a pauper lived there who was classed as infirm.

Green Corner must have been at the end of Hobman Lane, Hoggleman as it would be called then. Here lived Simpson Anderson, joiner and wheelwright, with his family, his father of 92, and two apprentices living in. At that time all apprentices lived in, were bound to their employers and suffered severe penalties if they stepped out of line, as W Scruton found to his cost.

Then we go to the top of Cranswick Street, where what is now known as Manor Farm was then Gannock or Ganwick. Across the High Road was Kell Cottage, occupied by William Goodlass, joiner. Later it became a blacksmith's shop run by the Sissons family until about 1918.

Opposite Burn Butts road end was the old hostelry, coaching inn and farm, the Denisons' Arms. This must previously have been the Decoy Inn, as the Directory of 1823 mentions William Bolton of the Decoy Inn, and the 1851 census records them as both being on the High Road, though there has never been any other public house there, except the Denisons' Arms, Londesborough Arms or the New Inn, as the old place has been called over the years. It lost its licence about the beginning of this century, when a couple called Fisher were the proprietors. Here was Timothy Barmby, publican and farmer of 25 acres.

South Hall, 737 acres, was farmed by 60 year old John Catton. He employed thirteen servants; of these two were domestic, the rest worked on the farm. One of these, twelve year old Seth Walker, was described as a cowherd.

To go back down the Main Street, at Ivy House Farm was Jonathan Dunn, farmer of 320 acres, who employed seven servants; two of these were employed in the house (one was only 12 years of age), and the rest were employed on the farm.

Next to the railway, at the premises now occupied by Foreman's was George Metcalf, joiner and wheelwright, with a family of two and a 17 year old apprentice.

A machine maker, William Allison, lived near or in Robin Hood Row, though what kind of a machine maker we are not told.

William Bowes, senior, and William Bowes, junior, both blacksmiths, lived next door to one another nearby.

Then came Sheepman Lane where Hannah Blythe and her son John farmed 21 acres. It is now owned by John Clare.

George Hobson, 72, of Sheepman Farm (a native of Cranswick) was classified as a freeholder and occupying ten acres. Sheepman Farm was always known locally as 'Boggle Hall' because it was supposed to have a ghost which rolled chamber pots down the stairs. One man who was born in a house in Sheepman Lane, (that house has long since been demolished) always said that there was something sinister about the old place. At that time there were a lot of trees in the lane, and on a dark night a good imagination could place all sorts of tricks. However, one night in March 1941, one of Hitler's planes dropped a bomb in the foldyard. The yard was empty at the time and so was the house, though it was damaged beyond repair and was later pulled down. That may have exorcised the old ghost, or he may have moved a mile or so across to the road between Watton and Cranswick and joined forces with the wicked Abbess Hilda from Watton Abbey. Her torso is supposed to float over the fields near the High Road, though nobody has actually seen it.

Then to Southgate, where there were three empty houses. Here were more of the Sandersons: George; 42, master tailor, his sons George and Ralph, also tailors, and one apprentice. Another George, 64, was also a tailor, though his son, 22, was a cobbler.

Elizabeth Dawson, 57, widow, farmed Ellis Grange, 158 acres in Southgate, with the help of her two sons and two daughters, and two hired lads aged 17 and 13. The old house and farm buildings were knocked down a few years ago to make way for building development. Part of the land now belonging to Highfield Farm, and some now owned by the Parish Council were then farmed from Ellis Grange.

At Green End, which seems to have been the top end of Southgate, was another Sanderson, John, a tailor, nearby was Edmund, also a tailor.

Sunderlandwick, Poundsworth and outlying farms of the Parish

Sunderlandwick Hall was owned by E H Reynard, who was born at Ripon and was classified as landed proprietor and Justice of the Peace. F Reynard, his son, was two years old. Quite a few people will remember him; he was usually known as 'Auld Freddy'. He was never very popular, and when he got control of the estate, often tried to assert himself as the so-called Squire, though in brushes with the local population he often came off second best. He usually wore a monocle, which did not improve his appearance, and always rode a horse. The postmaster at Cranswick, when he saw Fred Reynard ride by, used to stick a halfpenny in one eye, glower across at him and make a few rude remarks. I suppose 'Auld

Freddy' would wish he had the power to have him hanged, drawn and quartered.

At the hall there were twelve servants living in, who would be engaged by the year. The top wage would probably be £17 per year. The youngest would get less than half of that. Indeed the whole wage bill for the year would not be much more than £150.

Poundsworth Mill (the name suggests the customer got value for money) did a big trade in corn in the nineteenth century. It was also a farm of 320 acres and employed ten labourers. A boy of 12 was entered as an errand boy, and, like many more, would be employed a 'meart for work' basis and would get a shilling or two a week if he behaved himself.

Mary Dawson, 65, was head of the household, and ran the place aided by her two sons, both born at Poundsworth. The milling business came to an end before the end of the nineteenth century and the old mill was demolished a few years ago. There was a Thomas Dawson at Riverhead in Driffield, and Hutton in 1823. In 1840 there was still a Thomas Dawson at Hutton Mill, yet by 1851 he had vanished completely. He may have been one of the same family as there is an enormous tomb in Hutton chruchyard with just one inscription on the top: 'Sacred to the memory of Thomas and Mary Dawson, and their grandchildren of Poundsworth in this Parish.

Mary Dawson moved to Bechwood, the big house on the outskirts of Driffield where she died in 1873 aged 87 years and was interred in the big tomb in Hutton churchyard, as was her son Richard Dunn Dawson, also of Beechwood, who died two years later. There is no record of a Thomas Dawson being buried at Hutton. In 1738 Thomas Dawson of Poundsworth married a Mary Hornby of Driffield. They may be the Thomas and Mary whose names are inscribed on the tomb. There was also a George Dawson, a prominent Baptist, and in 1788 converts were baptised in the stream near Poundsworth Mill.

Rotsea, Corpslanding and Cranswick Common

Thomas Holtby and his brother Robert farmed both Rotsea farms of 300 acres each and had six domestic servants. The Holtbys finished farming Rotsea in 1926. At Corpse Landing was John Dalby farming 300 acres and employing eleven labourers. Later the Dalby family lost all they had and were reduced to working on farms for a living. William Blythe was farming Cranswick Grange, or Hutton Common as it was sometimes called. An old farming family, they were farming at Rotsea in the middle of the seventeenth century.

John Kirby farmed Cranswick common. The Kirbys were there until just before the First World War. At Little Common was Michael Barmby, farming 84 acres, and a native of Cranswick. His niece, daughter and father lived with him. Father was entered as a castrator. I remember my father telling a tale that when the Parish Council were accepting nominations for candidates (this would be about the beginning of this century), the clerk had a list of them and their occupations, which he proceeded to read out. Somebody had put their occupation as castrator, maybe as more of a joke than anything else. The clerk came to this word, seemed to boggle at it, then as it were took a running jump at it and bawled it out at the top of his voice, much to everyone's amusement.

Scurf Dyke, 380 acres, was farmed by 29 year old John Grainger. He employed seven labourers. All these farms which once employed seven or ten men, nowadays need only two or three. Sometimes one man can do all the work required in a week of 40 hours (with a little overtime at seedtime and harvest), where those workers of the mid-nineteenth century would work nearly double that time. This same John Grainger was one of the seven who signed the Infant School Certificate, in 1845, and was probably one of the farmers who helped to prepare this site.

Cranswick Main Street to J Hodgson's shop, Hutton Road and Hutton.

At the bottom of Hutton road in the narrow part at the junction of Main Street, lived Thomas Escritt, sometimes called the Bishop of Cranswick. This house has been used as a cowhouse for many years and is typical of the houses many of the countrymen lived in. There were usually one or two rooms below and a loft reached by a ladder. The loft was not always used as a bedroom; it was sometimes used for storage purposes. Three or more in a bed were quite common and 'hevving ti ger oot a bed ti ton ower' was not far from the truth. Anyway, it was a good way of generating heat on a cold winter's night.

When the older children got to 11 or 12 they were usually 'hired off', and that eased the pressure somewhat. The bedrooms in some of these old houses often had a beam across about breast high, or sometimes lower. In a few of these houses still standing there are beams which look as though they had been chopped straight out of a wood or a field hedge. There is just a flat side where the beam has been sawn out. The other side has had the bark knocked off, and that is about all. It almost looks as if the joiner of 200 years ago had said to the apprentice 'Gan inti that field and cop us a bit off that three (= tree).' Of course he would not do that, as all the timber would be well seasoned before use. There was often no money for house repairs, and some of the windows seem to have been the original ones. Often a family had occupied a house for 100 years, and no new windows had ever been installed. Yet when they were taken out they were as sound as when they were put in all those years ago.

Just across the road from Tom Escritt was William Denton, a farmer of 36 acres whose son Stephen, fifteen, was classed as a scholar. He must have been destined for higher things, as most children then left school at ten or twelve. Some of the women folk were entered in the census returns as dressmakers or seamstresses, as they were sometimes called. At this time when most of the clothes were made in the village, the dressmakers and tailors would usually have plenty of work.

At the Cross Keys was Richard Gowthorpe, 65, who was described as a publican brewer. He was born at Cottingham though his wife, Sara, was a native of this village. There was a family of three: Sara, 24, dressmaker, Richard Blythe, 22, and William, 16, apprentice druggist. They had a domestic servant 11 years of age living in. Another example of child labour. The shop next door, now a fish shop, was run by Robert Macdowell.

Christopher (Kit) Pearson, tailor and draper, must have lived at the shop opposite the green, how a hairdresser's. He was an expert fiddler and played in the choir of the Primitive Methodist church for many years. John Hodgson's tailor's shop was near and could have been the one run by Mrs Arnell which was bombed during the last war. Before we leave Cranswick it is worth while noting that the police constable, 33 year old Jacob Gibson, lived near Hodgson's shop. Sir Robert Peel's improved police system was introduced in 1839, yet according to the Driffield Times of 1860, Hutton Cranswick still had four parish constables.

Now back to Hutton Road, which was then called Main Street, and extended from the bottom of Hutton Road, through Front Street (now called Church Street), down Howl Lane to Low Green. There it was Back Street, including Mill Street, up to Balk Lane. The powers that be, in their wisdom, decided a few years ago that Back Street should revert to its old name of Orchard Lane. Where they got that from nobody seems to know, even those who have lived here all their lives and their fathers and grandfathers before them. Of course, the more snooty name of Orchard Lane fits in better with our increasing suburban image.

In the old Twin Towns Row, as it used to be called, which was knocked down a few years ago, were a gardener, a joiner and a wheelwright, with a few others of diverse occupations. At Hutton Mill was John Lawnsey, or Lawnsay (the name is nearly illegible). When the windmill was built is a bit of a mystery. On the Enclosure Map of 1770, where the mill now stands there was just a field, yet in 1823 there was a mill at Hutton run by Thomas Dawson. A mill in a village was essential, whether wind or water, and there is no record of one in or near Hutton Cranswick before the one at Hutton was built. The nearest would be Poundsworth, Watton or Beswick. So we must assume that the mill was built in the early years of the nineteenth century.

The last time a sail was renewed was about 1913 just before the First World War. After that same war the sails were dismantled and an oil engine installed. One time, during a high wind, the sails got out of control, whizzed round until one of them came off and ended up in the chalkpit across the road.

The mill and the 20 acres of land that went with it was the property of Reynards of Sunderlandwick until bought by A Proctor in 1926. When it was sold in 1955 the milling business ended. During the last war the top of the old mill was often used by the military for observation purposes.

At the farm, 60 acres, next to the mill was Hannah Parker and her son. Then we come to Front Street, or Church Street as it is now called. Here were a grocer, Amy Singleton, and a blacksmith, Thomas Martindale, with two sons, also blacksmiths. Their smithy would be at the junction of Church Street and Balk Lane, where two generations of Pearsons carried on the business until 1936.

At Manor House, opposite the telephone box, was Francis Jennison, who farmed 134 acres and employed six labourers. Opposite was Jubilee Farm. The house has just been demolished. Then it was called the Board Inn, though the name may have been changed later. These old pubs sometimes altered their names, and some of them were often very uncomplimentary. Their clients were usually more interested in the quality of the ale they drank and couldn't care less about what was on the sign over the doorway.

Eleven years earlier there were also two beer houses in Hutton. Now, in 1851, these seem to have gone. At this time the proprietor of the Board Inn was Catherine Goodlass, assisted by her son. They also farmed 12 acres.

Across the road at the vicarage was Beverley born Rev. Joseph Rigby, and at the bottom of Howl Lane was a horsebreaker.

In Back Street (now Orchard Lane) was Robert Stockdale farming 28 acres, and his son James, a wheelwright. The Stockdales were here for quite a while in the last century and probably the one before as joiners and wheelwrights. A James Wilkinson, 79, farmed 120 acres and employed two labourers. Elm Tree Farm was farmed by William Humphreys. He had a rather larger family than usual, seven.

John Fletcher lived in the house at the bottom of Church Lane where it meets Mill Street, and William Parker carried on his trade of shoemaker at the house near the churchyard in Church Lane.

I can remember many of the old people who used to call Mill Street Catto Street. There was a perfectly good reason for this: at the beginning of the present century at the top end of Mill Street and where a row of houses now stand there was a row of large hawthorne trees. Catto is the name for the fruit of the hawthorn. I can just remember these trees being cut down.

At this time there were in the parish:

Plumber and glazier	1
Shoemakers and cordwainers	10
Tailors and drapers	7
Wheelwrights	9
Blacksmiths	7
Grocers	4
Coal merchants	5
Tea Dealers	2
Carrier	1
Joiners	3
Millers	2
Chimney Sweep	1
Cobbler	1
Bricklayer	1
Roper	1
Machine Maker	1
Sempstress	1
Dressmakers	4
Schoolmaster	1
School Teacher	1
Mill setter	1

There were also 203 agricultural labourers and a few shepherds. 50 farmers and farmers' sons, as well as 24 paupers, one of whom was only 30 and blind, and an essential member of the community, one horsebreaker. (Today there are 23 farm workers in a parish of the same size and an equal number of farmers and their sons.) (These are all approximate figures). Strangely enough there was no saddler. There was not one in the village until the turn of the century when Robert Wilkinson set up in business in an old cottage where the Foresters' Hall now stands. Most villages of any size usually had a saddler to mend all the harness, stuff all the collars and keep the horses working in the fields and on the roads.

Ten years later, in 1861, the foundation stone of the Wesleyan Chapel was laid. Two cavities were left in which were placed two bottles, one containing the names of the ministers, trustees and architect, and in the other were placed copies o the Watchman, Methodist Recorder and the Driffield Times. Trustees were Mr Mark Foley and five others, all from Driffield. Some of the old village names among the builders were W Parker, Gowthorpe and Weatherall.

The Primitive chapel was built in 1854 at a cost of £700. It had on its front a clock of considerable size. Here is what J H Woodcock, author of *Piety among the peasantry*, says about it:

> Rev. J Shepherd was told by a man in the street that Squire Nicholson of Watton Grange, who along with his family used to attend the Sunday Services, had promised to pay three-thirds (sic) of the cost of the clock. The rest to be contributed by the railway company and public subscription.

The Chapel was demolished not long after it attained its centenary, and a house now stands on the site.

CHAPTER THIRTEEN

LATE VICTORIAN AND EDWARDIAN DAYS

In 1874 at the Driffield hirings young foremen were being engaged for £25 to £30 a year. This would be single men living in. Wags (wagoners) went for £18, boys £13 to £18, so states the Driffield Times. The young lads 'fost year off' would get about half that amount.

The Education Act was now operating and though compulsory schooling was not really effective until 1880, most of these lads would be 14 and over, so in some way the days of child labour were passing.

A shop in Driffield was selling Knights Heartburn Cakes, which cured (among other things) heartburn, acidity of the stomach, nausea and flatulence. There were many testimonials from the nobility.

That same year another kind of Domesday Book was compiled, giving a list of landowners, their acreage and the yearly value. Here are a few from this village:

Mercy Fletcher, Hutton	5 acres	£15 . 0s . 0d
Mathew Hobson, Cranswick	27 acres	£48 . 10s . 0d
John Hodgson, draper, Cranswick	2 acres 3 roods	£17 . 0s . 0d
George Sanderson, Cranswick	4 acres 2 roods	£45 . 10s . 0d
Rev Pudsey, Hutton	46 acres	£91 . 0s . 0d
W Barker, Hutton	2 acres 30 perches	£21 . 0s . 0d

Sir Tatton Sykes of Sledmere owned 34,011 acres, valued at £35,870. My own grandfather, who lived at Southburn, owned 1 acre, which was valued at £12. Here we have a wide difference in value between the large landowner and the small freeholder, or tradesman with his few acres.

Here is another extract from the Driffield Times of 1874:

A pullet belonging to Mr James Turner of Cranswick started to lay three weeks ago, and laid an egg every day except one. After that omission it laid two eggs per day for three days.

We are not told what kind of hen it was: like most layers of that time it was probably a mixture of many breeds. They scratched around in the mud and the muckheaps, roosted in the wagon sheds, brought up chickens under the hedgerows, and cost very little to keep. They usually lived to a ripe old age before finishing up in the pot. As one Cranswick man said, eyeing up a persistent broody, 'Ahl tell ma missus ti pur a bit a paest roon thoo' (paest = paste).

About this time American wheat was coming and forcing down the price of corn. It dropped from 54s. 8d. a quarter in 1870-75 to 35s. 8d. ten years later. By 1894 it was down to 22s. 6d.

In the early 1880's my father was walking nearly three miles each way morning and night. He set out for work at 5.00 am and was on the job at 6.00, and left for home at 6.00 in the evening like the workers thirty years earlier. For this he received the princely sum of 10s. a week. He often talked about a man who was out of work all winter and lived on nothing but swede turnips; neither did he steal them but got permission to take them from a farmer's field.

Farming at this time was feeling the pinch and in 1883 Sunderlandwick Estate had Slaper Leys, Gawdy Hall, Highgate and Sunderlandwick Farm were all to let. Highgate always had the reputation of being a poor farm, and Reynards were not very good landlords. One of the tenants at Highgate who had a poor harvest started to cart corn out of one of Reynards' fields. Freddy Reynard took a dim view of this and the offender had to leave.

The farm at the bottom of Mill Street, Hutton, was once tenanted by a man who could not pay his rent, and Reynards were going to sell him up to get it. The tenant's son worked on a farm a few miles away and his employer found out about this, so he sent the son one night during the hours of darkness with three horses and a wagon and told him 'Thoo wants ti an on that igh roard an up them grass fields an ger as much as thoo can ger on'. He went to the sale the next day and overheard Reynard's steward say, 'that's the old sod that did us'. Nothing could be proved, so he couldn't do anything. They may not have been very good times for the landlord, but unlike his tenant, he didn't face bankruptcy.

Another of the tenants got a notice of assessment from the Inland Revenue. He duly filled in the appropriate form and returned it. In due course an official returned with the form and said, 'You've put Outgo down as well as Income and there isn't a place for it'. The farmer replied, 'Ah know thur int; ah meard yan (= made one). Official: 'But your Outgo exceeds your Income'. Farmer: 'Ah know that an ahs gerrin oot'.

About this time Luke White of Driffield (later Sir Luke) was advancing money on security of freehold property. He was a solicitor, a very respected figure and was once Liberal MP for this district. Later he got into difficulties with his clients' money, and I believe he ended up in the workhouse, a completely discredited figure. Several people in this village lost money through him.

Here are some of the tradesmen and farmers in Cranswick in 1879:

Joseph Blythe	Farmer
William Blythe	Farmer
William Bowes	Blacksmith
John Catton	Farmer (South Hall)
Robert Dossor	Grocer
Mathew Hobson	Farmer (Sheepman Farm)
Henry Moore	Farmer (Burn Butts)
George Sanderson	Tailor
John Spink	Blacksmith

Henry Watson, brewer and bricklayer, kept the White Horse, and Mrs Sara Potter the Cross Keys

And in Hutton

Jesse Barker	Shoemaker
Thomas Hill	Carrier
William Jackson	Farmer and shopkeeper
James Moate	Farmer
William Pearson	Blacksmith
John Sissons	Farmer and Joiner
Charles Watson	Farmer and Bricklayer
Thomas Sissons	Joiner

The Bishop of Cranswick

According to the Parish Register, Thomas, son of William and Hannah Eskeret, was born at Cranswick on 7 October 1798. Why it should have been entered as Eskeret nobody will ever know. But this was the Tommy Escritt most of us have heard about, at least those who are natives of Cranswick, though they are getting fewer. Eskeret may have been the fault of the curate, Rev. J. Stanley, or it may have been some old name which has changed over the years. In a less bureaucratic age nobody bothered much about Deed Polls. The story of Tom Escritt is unique. You might travel all over England and never find one similar.

He was a remarkable man; when eighteen, he entered the service of Mr Moore of Burn Butts as a farm worker. That would be just after Waterloo, and he remained there (with the exception of two years) for nearly sixty. Those two years he was away he had a job in Leeds as a warehouseman. Though master and man parted with no acrimony on either side, there was an assurance from Mr Moor that his old job would always be waiting for him should he return. So after two years Tom came back to his native village, and his old job, saying he was glad to be 'hoam'. In going to his work in the morning and back in the evening it was said he walked over 150,000 miles, though this may have been something of an exaggeration.

Burn Butt is about two miles from Cranswick, and in those days they would start work at six o'clock in the morning until six at night. That was for a six day week. In harvest time they worked all hours, and sometimes by moonlight. I have often heard people talk about Tommy Escritt and his footprints, but nobody seemed to know much about the man himself. I was under the impression that he was a Baptist, but found on delving into his history that he was a Primitive Methodist, and a zealous one too. He even conducted Bible Classes at seven o'clock on a Sunday morning.

When Mr Moore was taken ill (though the Moores were staunch Anglicans), he didn't want the Vicar, only Tom to sit with him in his last days. Mr Moore died in 1864, and Tom was one of the chief mourners - an impressive figure with his long white locks.

At Mr Moore's death Tom asked to be buried as near his old master as possible and he is buried exactly at the feet of his old employer, just outside the iron railings around the Moores' burial place in Hutton churchyard. Though I have often walked by the Moores' burial place I never knew there was a memorial stone to Tom Escritt. However, I found it, cleaned it up a bit and the lettering is in quite good condition. He died on 15 January 1885 aged 87 years. His wife died in July 1875.

Tom Escritt in appearance was said to be of medium height, a kind of patriarchal figure. Miss Moore said that though he was no writer, and his principal reading was the Bible, his preaching was most impressive. At the opening of the Primitive Methodist Chapel at Cranswick, which was built in 1854, he gave an impassioned address.

In later life he went rather deaf, but he worked for the Moores as long as he could. When he could no longer walk to Burn Butts, they supplied him with food from their own table and looked after him to the end of his days. One morning when Tom Escritt was a young man going to work, and having left his wife at home ill, he stopped on the roadside to pray. This he did every morning and night for fifty odd years.

Those footprints are now buried beneath the Cranswick airfield. They were there in the thirties, and in the last years of Tom Escritt's life the Methodists held services there, and the Moore family attended.

I never knew where Tom Escritt lived until a neighbour, whose mother remembered him, said that he lived in a little house at the bottom of

Hutton Road which has long been used as a cowhouse, and where he probably died.

According to the 1851 census, he lived there with his wife and three children aged six to nine years; William Dee, lodger and shoemaker; John Foster, also lodger and railway porter; and Sarah Deighton, 75 years of age, blind and on parish relief, and no relation. She was probably someone whom Tom had taken in to save from the poor house just round the corner. His wage at that time would be about seven shillings a week.

During his 87 years Tom Escritt would have seen many changes. He lived through the Napoleonic Wars and the depression which followed. He saw the opening of the Hull to Bridlington railway in 1846, and the last of the stage coaches travelling on the High Road. And he saw changes in his own industry, agriculture: from the scythe, or 'ley' as he would call it, to the old put-off and sail reaper and later the binder, from the old flail to the threshing machine, but he would never think that years later planes would roar over the place where he stood and prayed for over half a century. Perhaps he still strides the lanes between Burn Butts and Cranswick in spirit.

The Rev. Henry Woodcock, in his book *Piety among the Peasantry*, tells of the Methodist stalwarts of the last century as he knew them. Tom Escritt was one of these. In fact he had a great deal in common with Henry Woodcock, who was born at Bridlington in 1830 and worked for a short time with a printer. Later he was apprenticed to a tailor. Wishing to enter the ministry, his master released him from his apprenticeship. He started with the Primitive Methodists as a local preacher, and as a minister was stationed twice at Driffield. He wrote five books in all. The poem which now follows is taken from Rev. Woodcock's book.

Tom Escritt's Poem 1875

In winter's cold I've had to tramp
Midst drifting snow and drenchin rain;
With hedges high and gypsies camped
And sheltered in Burn Butts lane.

And in the more reviving spring
I've travelled on from day to day,
Till the peewit on her wing
Bespoke the winter gone away

Cold winter gone, the hopeful thrush
With voice melodious and clear,

Sang sweetly in the hawthorn bush,
So welcome to the traveller's ear.

Now summer came when days were long
And the sun shone bright and clear,
When the lark repeats her song
And the pretty birds appear.

Across the fold she twittering flies
(In the English tongue called swallow)
She's crossed the seas by instinct ties,
The waters deep or shallow.

And in the pleasant month of June
When cuckoo cry in early morn,
The little warblers sang their tune,
The traveller only seems forlorn.

The middle part of the poem is missing, but it tells of the thousands of miles Tom Escritt walked between Cranswick and Burn Butts and then continues:

But soon my travels they must end,
Like those that's left the world before
I must into the grave descend,
And travel to Burn Butts no more.

That's a place endeared to me,
Through length of time and favour found
And though a poor old man I be
Their kindness more and more abounds.

Fifty three years have passed away
That length of time I've laboured there,
It seems like yesterday
When past with present I compare.

Some say that I'm a good old man,
While others they say no;
But I must do the best I can
I'm sure to reap what here I sow

And when I bid this world adieu,
And be as though I had been not,

I hope, dear friends, to meet with you
Where every sorrow is forgot.

From the parish magazine, 1895:

February 1895. Vicar Rev. O'Callagan.

Classes for laundry work were held every Friday from 2 - 4 o'clock in the Oddfellows Hall. The first classes were held on January 18th. A demonstration was given by Miss Wilson. Also on the 4th, 7th and 10th. Evening Classes were to be held on the 1st and 22nd and were open to the public.

We are not told much about the laundry classes, but of one thing we can be quite sure, there would be no detergents which make everything whiter than white, as the adverts would have us believe today. Could there have been a washing machine used similar to the one R. Tate of Driffield was advertising earlier in the century? I think it would all be done manually by the old dolly tub and peggy stick method. In most villages the washing machine was not widely used until after the Second World War.

March 1895

The vicar had received form Lord Hotham £10, his annual contribution to the Hutton Cranswick Coal Fund. To this had been added £1 from Mrs Beckitt, Watton Abbey. This was her annual Christmas contribution to the poor of the village. About 22 tons of coal had been distributed to fifty-six families, in quantities varying from five to ten hundred-weights.
Mrs Beckett had sent the vicar a second donation of the same amount in consequence of the severe weather, and two residents in the village had given him donations of 5s. and 10s. respectively. 27 tons of flour and 13 $\frac{1}{2}$ pounds of tea had been allocated to 27 families. A cheque for £2 from a friend in Driffield and 10s. from a parishioner, had been used to alleviate the more urgent cases of need.

Judging by this, quite a large proportion of the population were receiving aid in some form or another. Dr Clark's lectures on horticulture continued to draw large audiences. One night the attendance was nearly 200. That same month a new School Board was elected comprising :

W Gill	Stationmaster
Rev O'Callagan	Vicar
W Jackson (snr)	Shopkeeper
W Sanderson	Postmaster
T Hobson	Farmer
J Turner	Shoemaker

June 19th was the anniversary of the Foresters, usually known as Feast Day. This was a big event in village life. On this occasion the usual service was held in the Parish Church, where a collection was made on behalf of the Driffield Cottage Hospital which realised 10s. 6d. The dinner was provided by Mrs Poole of the Pack Horse Inn, and Mrs Turner's large booth on the Green, in which the dinner was laid, was filled to its utmost capacity. The members of the Oddfellows who had previously attended a service at Watton Parish Church joined the Foresters at dinner.

According to the vicar, it was some years since the two societies had dined together on their anniversary, and he hoped it would continue in future years.

After dinner the usual loyal toasts were proposed and drunk. Alderman Luke White (later Sir Luke), and member of Parliament for Buckrose, the local constituency, attended. During the dinner the vicar castigated the large numbers of people who joined the processions to the Church and then remained outside during the service. It was not so much the discourtesy to the preacher (the Vicar of Market Weighton), but the dishonour done to God by those who remained outside, and he hoped there would be no repetition of it another year.

So said the vicar. He does not say whether anybody remained outside whilst the dinner was being disposed of, but I think we can take it for granted that none of the Society members would let the chance of a free meal slip by, whatever their religious scruples.

Probably some of those who remained outside the church were Methodists who wouldn't have gone inside at any price. At that time many of the Dissenters, or Ranters as they were sometimes called by the churchmen, were often at loggerheads with the church and the vicar. It was often said that the parson and the local squire ruled many of the villages in those days. It never happened here, as many of the people were self-employed and did not owe allegiance to anybody. If the parson or the nearest to a squire they possessed (Reynard of Sunderlandwick) said anything they thought was out of line, they immediately cut them down to size.

Though the Wesleyans and the Primitives more or less went their separate ways, they usually joined forces to slap the church down. At this time the Methodists' union was nearly forty years away.

I remember one man - this was before the First World War a staunch Wesleyan, saying 'Some foaks onny goas to choch sae a bit a glory ull drop on em off Reynards'. The same man heard his schoolgirl niece, whom he was bringing up, reciting some of the Church Catechism and found she was being taught it in the day school. He rushed round to the schoolmaster and told him it would have to stop. That was the end of that kind of teaching in the school. It seemed to be a case of 'Church is Church, Chapel is Chapel, and never the twain shall meet'.

The Methodists welcomed the down and outs (those who could not afford a Sunday suit), while the church was the place for the gentry, who did not like mixing with the ragged from the lower strata of society, such as the bullocky with his 'trousers cloamed up', or the 'wag' (wagoner) who smelt of stables. Neither did the church like the rip-roaring evangelism of the Methodists.

Rev. C.F. Morris, one-time vicar of Nunburnholme, in his book *Yorkshire Reminiscences,* tells a story of a farmer's son who was just a bit simple, or a bit 'easy'. He was a Methodist while the rest of the family belonged to the Church, which he called 'Jerryboams' Cauphoos' (calf house). He would pray aloud for an hour before going to bed. Here is some of it:

> Laud shak sinners, Shak em reet ower hell, give em a sniffter o brimsun an threacle, but deaarnt let em throp in. They've been ramming an knockin at hells frunt deear fit ti ram'd deear doon. Lawd, shak em ower hell awaal tha roar like a bull wiv a soor lug. Swizzen thur whiskers for em an then thall know what o'clock it is. (Swizzen = burn, scorch).

The Methodists certainly 'wakkened em up'. Nowadays the Church and the Methodists hold combined services, and the bigotry of those days is forgotten. In 1901 the Foresters' Hall was built on the site of some old cottages and was the venue for the Club Feast dinners.

Now a note from the Driffield Times, 1861:

The Foresters celebrated their 23rd anniversary in the Pack Horse. The Village has been formerly noted for its riotous conduct on Feast Day. This one was celebrated in an orderly manner.

From the parish magazine, 1909

The Charitable Society

> This Society held its annual concert and dance in the Foresters Hall on the evening of January Ist. The Hall was filled, and a dance followed which was enjoyed by the large company present. This was the third year the effort had been made in the parish, and was a success financially. There were sufficient funds in hand to enable the Society to make gifts to the widows and deserving poor of the Parish next Christmas. The preceding Christmas £10 was distributed, each widow received 5s., and each case of deserving poor 2s. 6d.
>
> The vicar said it seemed a small amount, but was most welcome to the recipients in the parish where poverty was so prevalent. He also hoped the Urban District Council (he must have meant the Rural) would asphalt the footpath leading to Cranswick. He said on a rainy day it resembled a shingly beach at the seaside. In winter it was a veritable quagmire. After references to prehistoric man and the undergrowth affording protection to his feet, the vicar lambasted the Council for not getting on with the job.

Suffice it to say that the vicar got the footpath asphalted not long after. So were the footpaths on both sides of Front Street (now Church Street). This aggrieved the Hutton villagers, especially the Nonconformists, who said these paths got preference because they led to the church, while the footpaths in Mill Street and Back Street never saw asphalt until after the Second World War.

Empire Day

> This day was observed by the children attending the day schools saluting the flag outside the school. and singing patriotic songs. In the evening they gave a concert in various national costumes, and the proceeds of £2.5s.0d was to form a nucleus of a fund for providing a piano for the school.
>
> The Club Feast was held on June 16th, when both Clubs united again. The special preacher was the Rev. O'Callagan, vicar of Mappleton. (The Rev. Wheatley was now the incumbent of Hutton.) At the dinner in the Foresters' Hall the vicar was

supported by Sir Luke White, Mr Mark Sykes (later Sir Mark), Messrs Duke, Holtby, H. Moore and others.

There is no mention of anyone staying outside the church during the service or otherwise annoying the vicar.

In his magazine the vicar bemoans the fact that, like many other parsons, he has to live in a house which is far too big and costly to run. Incidentally, he was a bachelor and lived to a ripe old age. After saying that but for the 'white elephant' of a house he might be in a more comfortable position, he goes on to say that many vicars have furrowed brows and prematurely whitened hair due to their battles with poverty. He ends with saying 'that the laity should try to alleviate the suffering of the clergy'.

What the vicar said about his large house was quite true. It was built in 1874 by Lord Hotham, who bore the whole expense, and was sold in 1965 to a private owner, while a smaller place was built nearby for the vicar's use.

A stranger once passing by the vicarage in a horse and trap, when motor cars were a rarity, asked who was living in the large house among the trees. On being, told it was the vicar he said, 'If iver thoo cums across a parson ah bet es allus stuck at back av a lot of threes'. Rather unkind to the vicar.

Regarding his poverty, it must be remembered that most of his parishioners were living on 15s. a week or less, and for those over seventy the Old Age Pension of 5s. had just commenced, so they could hardly be expected to help the vicar in his distress.

The same year the vicar, who held some glebe land on Skerne Road let as allotments, announced his intention of giving a couple of prizes to two tenants who farmed their land the best. Some non-resident would be selected as judge, who would have to be impartial. The vicar then launched into a long diatribe against those foolish persons who thought they could reap a crop without putting anything in the land. He thought his tenants would agree that the biggest curse was the individual who allowed his land to become full of rubbish, and allowed the seeds to be spread over his neighbours' lands. This kind of farmer, the vicar thought should be eliminated along with the weed he allowed to grow. All of which was sound common sense. What the reverend's prizes were and who got them I never found out. There is a kind of sequel to this, as a few years later, during the war years, one of the tenants had a good sale of clover and got rather a large cheque; foolishly he told the vicar, who promptly put up all the rents.

An old schoolfriend told me how his father went about the process of getting the tenancy of some of this land, most of which was free working and suitable for garden crops. His father was not a Church goer, but more of a Methodist, so all the family duly walked all the way from Cranswick to the church every Sunday. There was no getting out of it for the children. In those days father's word was law. In due course a piece of land became vacant; father got the tenancy and never darkened the doors of the church again. However, the vicar continued to visit him regularly and didn't seem to bear any animosity.

In spite of all his protestations of poverty, perhaps he knew that the produce of two or three acres of land made a great deal of difference to the standard of living of his parishioners. In those hardup days before the First World War even a shilling or two a week extra was always welcome.

THE EARLY TWENTIETH CENTURY

Tradesmen in the village in 1905:

Hutton:

J. Barker	Shoemaker
W. Dosser	Grocer
T. Fletcher	Market Gardener
W. Pearson	Blacksmith
D. Proctor	Miller
G. and J. Tate	Market Gardeners
J. Tindall	Joiner
C. Watson	Bricklayer and Farmer
G. Wilson	Carrier and Market Gardener

Cranswick:

S. Bowes	Blacksmith
D. Consitt	Carrier
C. and A. Dossor	Grocers
W. Duke	Bootmaker
J. Harvey	Market Gardener
R. Welbourne	Tailor
W. Jackson Jnr	Grocer
W. Jackson	Rate Collector
H. Lovell	Horse Breaker
J. Potter	Shoemaker
J. Robson	Hairdresser

E. Sanderson	Bootmaker
W. Sanderson	Post Office
G. Sissons	Joiner
J. Sissons	Joiner
T. Sissons	Blacksmith (Beverley Road)
R. Smith	Bricklayer
W. Spink	Blacksmith
R. Summerson	Joiner
W. Train	Horse Breaker
J. Turner	Shoemaker
G. Turner	Butcher
R. Weatherall	Rope Maker
R. Wilkinson	Draper and Saddler

The Case of Harry Savage

In every town or village there is always some mystery or tragedy which is never solved. We are often treated to the spectacle on radio or television of some amateur sleuth trying to unravel some long forgotten happening where all the principal figures have long since passed on.

Though it may have only been recorded by a line or two in the local press, the case of Harry Savage of Cranswick was never solved. The time would be somewhere before the First World War. He worked at Decoy Farm, Watton Carr, and like most of the workers of that era was living in.

One day in early October he got on the train at Cranswick to go to Hull Fair. and was never seen again. He just vanished from the face of the earth. I remember talking to a man who knew him that would be over fifty years ago and he said he saw him talking, or rather arguing, with some rough characters in a public house near the docks. That seems to have been about the last time he was seen. It may have been a case of murder, nobody knows, and as nearly seventy years have elapsed, it is doubtful whether anybody will ever know. So the case of Harry Savage may remain for ever on the file of unsolved mysteries.

George and Rachel

The turn of the century was supposed to be the heyday of the British Empire, but it didn't benefit the ordinary man, least of all the countryman. He still had to work long hours for a mere pittance. Take the case of George and Rachel Dickinson.

They both hawked coals with a donkey and cart, and lived in the end house of Prospect Row, Low Green. Hutton. Exactly how long they did it is obscure, but they were in business in the Nineties. George usually walked behind the cart hanging on to the 'hairbreed' as the stay on the back was called.

George died in 1908, aged 78. but Rachel carried on by herself for a few years longer. Coal was 11d. a bag and she charged 3d. for delivering 5cwt of coal, and 1d. more for shovelling it in. Five hundredweight would be about the load for a donkey to pull from the station round the village, as most of it is uphill. According to one of her descendants, many of whom still live in the village, she looked after her donkey very well.

When she gave up work, some time before the First World War, she went to live in a little house not far from the present W.I. Hall. I can remember seeing her knitting at the door of her cottage when I was going to school. She died about 1918 and must have been well over 80.

Life was getting just a little better, and in the last years of her life, she would draw the pension of 5s., and later 10s. a week, thanks to the great statesman Lloyd George. 10s. was a large sum in those days and helped the old people from being branded as paupers, or 'on the parish' as it was often called. Incidentally, the little corner, or 'nab end', in Howl Lane, or Howly as it was more often called, was always known as Donkey corner. This little plot where Rachel's donkey grazed and the children had their bonfire on Guy Fawkes Night is now covered by houses.

The Hothams

Now a contrast in styles of living to that which Rachel Dickinson and her compatriots, neighbours, or whatever you would like to call them, enjoyed or endured. There is no intention here to eulogise the Hothams. The ordinary inhabitants of this parish, but for an accident of birth, could have attained a place in history. Wasn't it the American humourist Mark Twain who said you couldn't be too particular about the parents you chose?

The Hothams were people of privilege, who were interrelated to all the most influential families in this country and who hobnobbed with Kings and Queens. They were also so much a part of the history of this parish that they cannot be ignored.

When William the Conqueror invaded England, his halfbrother, Count Mortain. fought with him at Hastings and receiving enormous tracts of land all over the country. The Count had two followers, Nigel Fossard and Richard de Surdoral. These two got most of his Yorkshire lands. In 1085 this Fossard, among other manors. held the Manor of Hode (Hotham). about 660 acres as well as a mill. The Normans drove out the Saxons who lived there and replaced them with their own retainers.

One of Fossard's followers was a knight called William, father of Durand-de-Houdhum. This William is supposed to be the first recorded ancestor of the Hothams.

Sir Geoffrey-de-Hotham, often called Sir Gilfred, was Lord of the Manor of Cranswick in the thirteenth century. Cranswick was the oldest manor belonging to the Hothams and was sold in 1908. F. Ross states that in 1315 a Galfredus-de-Hotham was Lord of the Manor of Hutton-cum-Cranswick. Even in the nineteenth century it was given that name in some directories.

Before the thirteenth century dawned, the Hothams had established themselves at Scorborough. They held this under the Percys, who were then at Leconfield Castle. John-de-Hotham was the first to take up residence there, though still under the age of twenty-one. Scorborough was in their possession until it was burnt down in the eighteenth century.

Then we come to the most famous of all the Hothams, especially in the annals of East Yorkshire, Sir John Hotham, the first Baronet, Governor of Hull and his son John, usually known as Captain Hotham. The elder Hotham was knighted in 1621 by James I. He also had five wives in twenty-eight years, and was returned as Member of Parliament for both Appleby in Westmorland and Beverley. He decided to sit for Beverley as it was nearer, and because he thought he could exercise more influence there.

During the Civil War, while Governor of Hull, Sir John turned his coat twice, was captured by the Parliamentarian troops in Beverley. Taken to London and imprisoned in the Tower. On 30 November 1644, Sir John was brought before a court martial at the Guildhall London. His son Durand of Lockington, who was a lawyer, conducted his defence, though to no avail, and he was condemned to be executed on 16 December.

Lady Hotham tried without success for a pardon, but only got a stay of execution until 24 December to give her husband time to settle his affairs. A Petition was sent to the Commons that Sir John's life should be spared, but after some wrangling between the Lords and the Lower House. it was dismissed and the execution was announced for 4 January.

As Captain Hotham, his son, had also been found guilty and was to be executed on 1 January, it was decided that the father should follow him to the block the next day. 2 January 1645, so Sir John Hotham died at the age of fifty-six and was buried in London.

Captain Hotham had three wives in thirteen years, and represented Scarborough in the Long Parliament. He seems to have been a more reckless character than his father, though they may both have been more sinned against than sinning. On 1 January 1645, at the age of thirty-five,

Captain John Hotham was to meet the executioner. Here is the historian A.W.M. Stirling's version of it:

> The night preceding the execution of the young officer, his wife Isabel, from whom he had been separated during his imprisonment, was allowed to visit him in the Tower. She quitted him only in the morning when he was led out to die. And in the dawning of that year, which to the one was to bring death and to the other bereavement, the sorrowful couple bid each other a last fare well. Nine months later Isabel gave birth to a son, Henry, but who, the child of tears and grief, sank to an early grave.

Brother Durand attended Captain Hotham at his execution. Like his father he was buried in London. When Sir John Hotham was arrested his property was confiscated, but after his death it was restored to John, the eldest son of Captain Hotham, with his Uncle Durand acting as guardian. It is interesting to record that this John Hotham in later life was, like his grandfather, appointed Governor of Hull in January 1689. He caught a chill while travelling from Hull to Beverley and died on 6 April the same year. Probably the Hotham who had more connections with this parish than any other was Durand, the son of the Sir John who died on the block. He may have lived at the Manor House, Front Street, Hutton. The date on the front says 1884, but that was the date when it was rebuilt. There will have been a Manor House there for centuries before that. Durand Hotham was appointed Justice of the Peace in 1649 after the Civil War was over, and was still in office in 1694. In the first years of Hutton Cranswick Parish Register every burial affirmation was underlined by an affidavit usually produced by a member of the family. At the year end all these were signed by Durand Hotham, who had probably issued them in the first place. He would also have to examine the circumstances of all deaths and ascertain whether there was anything suspicious.

He was a lawyer of no mean ability, and a friend of the Quakers, though history does not tell us whether he was one himself. Like all the other Hothams he seems to have been a staunch Protestant. George Fox, the founder of the Quakers, said he visited Justice Hotham at the Manor House, Cranswick, in 1651 and described him as being 'a pretty tender man.'

This was the time when Fox, hearing what he called 'a great high priest' preaching near Hutton Cranswick, shouted to him, 'Come down thou deceiver, dost thou bid people come freely and take of the water of life freely, and yet thou dost take £300 a year from them for preaching the Scriptures to them.'

However, in August 1908, all the estates in the Hutton Cranswick area were sold by auction. There were 841 acres of land and the farmsteads that went with them, also nineteen cottages in Hutton and Cranswick. Some of the farms and the cottages were bought by the sitting tenants, so after eight hundred years the Hothams relinquished all connection with this parish.

Field House, Hutton Road.

Main Road, Burn Butts Lane to the right.

Main Street with Cross Keys and Listers Stores c. 1900.

Main Street and White Horse Inn.

Wesleyan Methodist Chapel, Main Street 1953.

Interior of Methodist Chapel, Main Street.

White Horse and Cranswick Green, c. 1905.

Beverley Road, top of Main Street, c. 1974.

Main Street, towards Beverley Road, c. 1974.

Main Street with Cross Keys, c. 1974.

Cranswick Pond.

Cranswick Pond and Village School.

Odd Fellows Hall, c. 1905.

Cricket Square on the Green, c. 1910.

Southgate Chapel (now demolished), c. 1910.

Sandersons, back of the Green, c. 1920.

Old Church Rooms (demolished in 1998), c.1920.

CHAPTER FOURTEEN

THE RISE AND FALL OF THE LONDESBOROUGHS

Londesborough Park, in the village of Londesborough, near Market Weighton, with its large estates was bought by George Hudson, the 'Railway King', in 1846. In 1850 he went bankrupt and the house came into the possession of Albert Denison Conyngham, who was created peer in the same year. Albert Denison Conyngham had been practically penniless but had inherited a large fortune from his uncle, a Mr Denison. He had started life as a poor boy from Yorkshire who entered the banking world in London and rose to the top. Lord Londesborough complied with the will of his uncle and kept the name Denison only. He was a keen archaeologist and excavated a burial mound near Halimanwath Bridge, Driffield, in 1851. This site was where the Driffield to Market Weighton line, now disused, was to run forty years later. The same year he did some excavations on Mount Ararat, near Kings Mill, Driffield.

From the early part of the nineteenth century the Londesboroughs owned a considerable amount of land in this district; namely, the farm of Burn Butts, part of which is in Hutton Cranswick parish and the rest in Watton, and also South Hall, Bustard Nest, Scurf Dyke, Throstle Nest, Angram, Decoy, Standingholme and Topilow.

According to the entry in the Registry of Deeds, Lord Albert Denison bought various parcels of land in March 1850, the month in which he was created Lord Londesborough. The previous owners were George Hudson of Sewerby Park, Robert Buchanan Dunlop of Dunbartonshire and Sir Charles Rugge Price of London.

There were 737 acres of land, from gardens of fifteen perches to arable fields of 36 acres. There are many familiar names. We get South Hall, 2 acres 27 perches, and stackyard 2 acres 29 perches. The red South Hall was at the bottom end of Southgate in the field called Old Wires. This field, nearly six acres, was also included in the transaction. The South Hall on the Beverley to Driffield road was built by one of the Londesboroughs late in the nineteenth century.

Tinkler Kell field is recorded as Tinkler Knell. The clerk who wrote it may not have known that 'kell' means spring'. He may have thought someone named Tinkler had met a sticky end there. 'Rivieng On' is also listed. The locals always call this field 'Rarving On', as it is very tough land. It now belongs to Cranswick Common Farm. The old toll bar, 16 perches, on the Beverley to Driffield road is included. East Woodrams, or New Inn Field, 13 acres. Here again the name was spelt incorrectly, as this would be the Wotherams which was adjacent to Beverley road and stretched across what is now the old aerodrome.

Included in the sale were what were called 'parts of Cancar', four fields on the east of the parish. These four, 10, 17, 12 and 12 acres in extent, were put to South Hall; later they were sold off and are now part of Winneforth Farm. Bustard Chalk Pit field, 17 acres 3 roods, near the road leading to Burn Butts. All these are just a representative sample of the land Lord Londesborough bought in March 1850. At the end of the list in the Registry of Deeds is this statement:

> Tithes payable of all the Inclosures of Hutton Cranswick and parts of the Rotsea now commuted at rent charges of £14 and £22. Also an annual payment of £7 from Lord Hotham. Outgoings from the Hutton Cranswick Estate:
>
> | | |
> |---|---|
> | To the vicar of Hutton Cranswick | £5 |
> | For the benefit of poor widows | £2.10s.0d |
> | To poor apprentices | £2.10s.0d |
> | The Dean and Chapter of York | £1.14s.0d |

People who remembered the Londesboroughs in their heyday said it was entertaining Royalty which dissipated most of their fortune. No doubt this was true, as the Prince of Wales, later King Edward VII, was entertained at Londesborough, as this extract from the National Farmers' Union Journal of 1977 describes one visit:

> On January 26th, 1882, the Prince of Wales, who was then staying at Brantinghamthorpe, the home of one of the Sykes family, alighted from the train at Kiplingcotes station for a day's shooting on the Londesborough Estate. Lord Hotham had the little station decorated with crimson cloth, bunting and plants, and the Royal Standard was surmounted by a triumphal arch. Several wagon loads of schoolchildren were drawn up nearby. These with the local inhabitants gave hearty cheers as the Prince stepped from the platform. He was said to have been pleased with the decorations and reception. Later he enjoyed an excellent day's shooting.

There were four visits by the Prince of Wales to Londesborough. The last was in 1905 when he was King Edward. George V also visited Londesborough in 1902 when he was Prince of Wales. The second Lord Londesborough, who inherited a rent roll of £100,000 and two million in stocks and shares, must have had a positive dislike of money. He threw it about as if it was of no account and what was spent at these jamborees when Royalty was entertained is almost beyond belief. These were the great days of the Victorian and Edwardian eras. Great for the Londesboroughs and the Hothams, not so much for the lower classes of society, as the majority of the populace were called, those who just existed and worked all their lives for a few shillings a week. The Londesboroughs may have regretted their association with the rakish Prince of Wales, who seemed to have the morals of a tom cat, as their fortunes must have been on the wane in 1909 when the Skerne estate of about 3,000 acres was sold in October of that year. The estates in 1883 were all in the three ridings of Yorkshire and amounted to 52,655 acres with a gross rental of £67,876. Today these estates would be valued at many millions. The second Earl, 1864 - 1917, left unsettled estates valued at £303,982. Lord Londesborough also owned a large estate near Scarborough. The Londesborough downfall was hastened by two deaths, that of the second Earl in 1917 and his son in 1920. The estates then passed to the 3rd Earl's brother, Hugo. The subsequent death duties were the precursors of large land sales.

One of the Londesboroughs married a Sitwell of Scarborough, the family whose home near Valley Bridge was bought by Scarborough Corporation and has been open to the public for many years. Edith Sitwell, born at Scarborough in 1887, who wrote Collected Poems and an autobiography, as well as other works, often did her shopping in Market Weighton.

In 1921 there were 6,000 acres of the Londesborough Estate for sale. There was land in many parts of the East Riding, some near Market Weighton. In this district there were Scurf Dyke, Throstle Nest, Angram, Decoy, Standingholme and Topilow. These farms were bought by private buyers. The Eagle Inn at Skerne was sold for £560, which must have been a good price. A great deal of this land was withdrawn and, as the great depression of the 20s and 30s was just beginning, helped by the repeal of the Corn Production Act in 1921, this land would be difficult to sell at any price. South Hall and Burn Butts, once part of the Londesborough Estate, were sold to the occupiers not long before the First World War. What remained of the estate was sold in 1923.

There is now no Earldom of Londesborough, as this title was extinguished by the failure of direct issue in the male line on the death of the last Earl in 1963. The Barony still remains and the present baron, Richard John Denison, born in 1959, succeeded to the title in 1968. (A Barony is the lowest rank in the peerage, above a baronet and below a

Viscount. Today an Earl or a Baron means nothing. A sweep or a dustman can hold either of these titles, even if he hasn't got a halfpenny.) The last of the Denisons, or Londesboroughs, now lives near Redditch in Worcestershire. There must be some money left from the wreck of their fortunes as he was educated at Wellington College, and is a member of the Thames Yacht Club, Henley. One of the Lord Londesboroughs, along with Lord Hotham, was Lord of the Manor of Hutton Cranswick. The Hothams kept their lands in this parish for nearly 800 years, though they lived in far more dangerous times than the Londesboroughs. The Hothams got most of their lands through the grace and favour of a monarch; a poor lad from Yorkshire founded the fortunes of the Londesboroughs. Today the only things to remind us of them is the road in Cranswick, recently named after them, the house in Southgate called Londesborough Lodge where their agent lived, and the farm houses of South Hall, Angram and Throstle Nest, which carry the Londesborough coat of arms.

THE REYNARDS OF SUNDERLANDWICK HALL

In 1812 Horner Reynard inherited the Horner's lands in Hutton Cranswick and Sunderlandwick. His son, Edward Horner Reynard, was born at Ripon in 1811. The family had an estate at Hob Green nearby. Edward Horner Reynard was residing at Sunderlandwick in the middle of the nineteenth century. His son, Fred Reynard, took over the estate on the death of his father. When Fred Reynard died in 1925 some of the estate was sold to pay off death duties. More was sold after the Second World War and the remainder was bought by Sir Thomas Ferens in 1957. Edward Horner Reynard and his son Fred may have been the only two to reside permanently at Sunderlandwick Hall. Fred Reynard's son, Claud, usually known as Major, acquired land in Kenya, formerly German East Africa, when the First World War ended. He spent most of his time there and left Sunderlandwick in the hands of a steward.

His son, Andrew, usually known as Andy, was a civil engineer and spent very little time at the Hall. During the last war it was taken over by the RAF when it caught on fire. Andy, who I believe was then living in Driffield, came to view the fire and was heard to say, 'That'll shift the buggers out'. After that, some of the Free French Army with American tanks trained there until they embarked at Hull for France in July 1944. There is a stained glass window in Hutton Cranswick installed by Mr and Mrs F. Reynard in memory of another son who was killed in the First World War.

CHAPTER FIFTEEN

FROM THE PARISH REGISTER

The Parish Register

Just names inscribed in a dusty, dingy book;
You might think not worth a second look,
Some, examples of a penman's art (like copper-plate);
Others as if they had been written with a grimy stake.

Yet still a history of our ancestors' village life;
Three hundred years of peace and war and strife.
Records of weddings and happy days long gone;
Memories of stalwarts who have since passed on.

Baptisms, nuptials, deaths, encompassing life's span;
Reminders that how fleeting are the years of man.
Some whose days could be numbered on one hand;
Others who lived far beyond their allotted span.

No village Hampden these pages do adorn
And no statesman, or general here was born,
Just cobblers, carpenters, bricklayers, and yeomen;
All simple, straightforward English countrymen.

Henry VIII is credited with ordering the institution of Parish Registers and I believe the earliest one in East Yorkshire dates from about the middle of the sixteenth century. Many did not come into being until over one hundred years later, when the Civil War with all its upheaval had come and gone. The historians tell us that during the Commonwealth all Registers were kept by a person duly appointed and not by the clergy.

The Register for this parish starts in 1653, and looking through these old books, some of the writing hardly legible, you are turning the pages of history, even if only local history.

Old names appear, their descendants with us today, as do tragedies long forgotten. The first recorded incumbent in the Register was the Rev. Ralph Mason. In 1640 there was a Ralph Mason who was vicar of Driffield, and an inspecting committee said of him: 'Mr Ralph Mason preaches at Great and Little Driffield after his fashion'. Evidently they were not impressed with his sermons. The Rev. Mason of Hutton and Driffield may have been one and the same man.

In that first year of the Register, Anne, daughter of John Reynolds, the 'registor' was baptised. He could not have been appointed by the Commonwealth. Usually the parson was the person who filled in the Register, which seems quite appropriate, as he had to officiate at all the Church weddings, baptisms and burials, apart from the fact that in some parishes he may have been the only person with any scholastic attainments.

'Henry Stork of Hutton, a sick seaman, came out of a man-of-war of the Queen's Fleet. Was half a year sick with his mother and was buried September 23rd, 1704.' This was one of the vicar's, the Rev. Thomas Hoggard, footnotes. What Henry Stork suffered from we are not told, nor why he lingered for six months at home.

Illegitimate children were entered frankly and brutally as the bastard child of so-and-so. Such a one was James, the illegitimate child of Ann Stork of Hutton, born on 23 January 1731. Ann must have been a member of the same family as Henry Stork. However, there was a happy ending, as four years later Ann married James Saunderson.

The vicar also records that the elm tree in the middle of Cranswick Green was planted by Thomas Dove and neighbours in 1744. The Doves were shopkeepers in Cranswick for over one hundred years.

About the same time another footnote says that a man named Coal had been killed in an accident between two wagons in Hobman Lane. The writing is black, smudged and hardly legible. Evidently there were traffic problems even in those days. The Coals, or Coles, were an old local family of yeomen farmers.

The last of the Coles were two old maiden ladies who lived in Front Street, Hutton, and died just before the First World War. Another tragedy: 'Robert, son of widow Cook, was killed 3 August 1732 by a fall from a wagon at bottom pit'. This would have been one of the Hutton chalk pits. Occupations mentioned in the eighteenth century register were tailor, sometimes spelt 'taylor', wright, shoemaker, weaver, blacksmith and shepherd. An entry for 27 March 1745 reads:

> At a vestry meeting it was agreed that William Stockton, William. Chambers, and Gaston Dove should set about acquiring a property for a poor house and report at the next vestry meeting.

The property which became the Poor House was the one occupied by Mr R. Milner and his father before him, and demolished a few years ago. This site, now built over, is opposite number 17 Main Street, Cranswick. Here is a selection of interesting entries from the register:

1760: Sir Charles Hotham, is recorded as having given 10,000 bricks from Lockington brickyard to build the churchyard wall. John Dillon, Matt Jenkinson, carpenter, Michael Nichol, bricklayer, and several other villagers helped to build it. (that wall is still in good condition today.)

1766: The vicar, after stating that the turnpike was set at Poundsworth Hook, says 'We had a very deep fall of snow on 29 April 1757. Another fall of snow the 6th June the same year'.

23 June 1766: Sara, the infant daughter of Richard Jenkinson of Hutton, had a fall out of a little girl's arms and died half an hour later. There was a coroner's inquest.

11 April 1768: Burial of Christopher Cooper, turnpike keeper at Driffield Beck. This was the toll collector appointed two years previously.

1769: Four old men said to be the oldest in the parish all buried between 12 October and 3 December. There is no mention of their ages.

1786: Bethel Robinson was the vicar and he records that John, son of G. Mosrain, was killed by a horse in a field; his arm was pulled off. What lies behind that bald statement we are not told, as very few horses would attack a man in such a manner as to pull an arm off. John Mosrain may have got himself entangled in some implement the horse was pulling. In those days surgery was practically non-existent and anyone in those circumstances would have met a miserable end.

16 October 1763: Ann, the daughter of William Chameron of Hutton, a Catholic, was buried without any ceremony. At this time Catholics, or Papists, as they were often called, were not very popular. J.H. Fletcher states: 'Catholics had to be married and buried by the ministers of the Established Church. A marriage by a Catholic priest meant a fine of £100, a burial incurred one of £20'.

In the seventeenth and eighteenth centuries many a devout Catholic was interred with no ceremony, and thereby hangs a tale, though it belongs to the present century. This came from an old acquaintance. A Catholic from Cranswick had just buried his wife. The year was 1900 and Catholic priests were then allowed to conduct services at the graveside. The wife of John - I omit his surname, as there are still descendants of his living in the village - was buried in Hutton churchyard by a Catholic priest from Driffield. Every week for three weeks after the funeral the priest turned up at the old man's home and asked for two or three shillings every time. This was supposed to help the transition of the wife's soul to the next world. At the end of the third week old John decided to pay no more and said: 'She let ti mak er orn roard noo'.

A few years later old John departed this 'vale of tears' and the same priest presided at the graveside. According to my informant, his brother was at the funeral acting in the dual capacity of bearer and mourner, as he had once worked for the old man. It was a day in August and the sky looked black as if a thunderstorm was imminent, the brother said it looked as it they were all going to get very wet. The priest said: 'Oh, it won't take long'. When the coffin had been lowered into the grave, the priest said a very few words in Latin, then threw two buckets of water over the coffin. As the priest got ready to depart he said: 'That will do for old John, he wasn't a very good Catholic and he didn't attend Mass often'. Just then the rain came down in torrents as he got into the hearse going back to Driffield.

> 13 August 1782: Another tragedy. James Norrington, servant to Miles Smith of Sunderlandwick, was killed in a chalk pit near Hutton. This must have been the one in Balk Lane, as this belonged to the Sunderlandwick Estate until 1926.

In the same year Jane Horsley died, aged 100. F. Ross records that Anne Jenkinson of Hutton Cranswick died aged 103 in 1816. This is not in the parish register. Whether all these figures could be substantiated is a different matter, though some could be proved to be authentic by the parish records.

In this parish very many died in infancy, but those who survived into adulthood seemed to become immune to most germs, and quite a few of them lived far beyond that 'three score years and ten', after which we are supposed to be on borrowed time. To use an old East Yorkshire expression: 'Tha wor as tearf as auld wickleather'. I have often heard this said about some of the old stalwarts, sometimes well on in their eighties, yet who could still work.

Another tragic note: G. Hought of Hutton Cranswick was killed by lightning on 4 August 1851, while sheltering under a tree during a thunderstorm. He left a wife and two children.

One of those who passed on in 1864 was W. Murphy, described as a mechanic. I wonder what sort of mechanic he would be, though as threshing machines had come to the East Riding in 1835, and reapers of different kinds followed later, I suppose anyone with a knowledge of these machines could have called himself a mechanic.

Another tragedy came in 1942 when seventeen-year-old Leslie Taylor, a keen Home Guard, was killed in a shooting accident in Hutton pit. These old pits seem to be singularly ill-fated.

The various incumbents who wrote these footnotes and performed the baptisms, weddings and funeral ceremonies, usually only gave the tragedies a little extra space in the register. These events would strike them more forcibly, but the happier events were seldom given in any detail. Still, they give us an insight into the living conditions of our forebears, though they often make rather gloomy reading.

CHAPTER SIXTEEN

EDUCATION BEFORE 1870

According to the Marriage Act of 1753 brides and bridegrooms had to sign their names, or if they were illiterate, to make their cross. In 1743 Thomas Dowbiggin, curate at Hutton Cranswick,, had reported:

> We have three places where children are taught, but not one school is endowed. The children there are not above forty in number. At present not thirty. The persons instructing them are careful to instruct them in the principles of the Christian religion, according to the doctrine of the Church of England.

The Directory of 1821 lists two school masters in the village: R. Richardson and Richard Vaukes. In 1865 the incumbents of different parishes were asked for their views on education. Here is the reply from the vicar of Hutton Cranswick, Rev. Pudsey:

> Alas there are three Chapels, the Independents, the Methodists and the Ranters places. The masses being steeped in poverty and ignorance frequent these schismatic displays as they would theatres.

Two of the chapels had just been built; Methodism was strong in the village; and men like Tom Escritt were probably reducing the vicar's congregation. As most of the church parsons of that time looked on the Methodists, Ranters, etc., with a jaundiced eye, they could hardly be expected to give an unbiased opinion.

Judging by the entries in the parish register from the early years of the nineteenth century, most of the couples getting married could not sign their own names and simply put a cross. By the middle of the century things were not much better: a slight improvement is to be detected in the Sixties. In the Seventies a bigger percentage could write their names. At the end of the century there were no more crosses in the register.

Official figures show that from 1839 to 1844 the men and women of the East Riding (with York) were only just behind London in literacy. The East Riding was a little superior to West Yorkshire.

Before compulsory schooling, Mary Simpson of Boynton Vicarage tried to help the hired farm lads of the district where she lived. She taught them to read and write during the evenings in the stables and farm buildings. Sometimes she followed them round the field when they were ploughing and sowing.

I can remember quite a few of those who received their education, such as it was, before the 1870 Education Act, and most of them could read and write reasonably well. There was only one I can call to mind who could do neither. Perhaps their literacy may have been due more to their own efforts than the limited schooling available.

George Crabbe, a poet of rural life and curate of Aldeburgh in the early years of the nineteenth century, tells how he tried to guide the hand of the bridegroom when signing the register. He says:

> Behold these marks uncouth,
> How strange that men who guide the plough
> Should fail to guide the pen.
> For half a mile the furrows evenly
> For half an inch the letters stand awry.

Many of the old schoolteachers of that era were nearly illiterate and often partly disabled war veterans. Sometimes they also acted as Parish Clerk and Rate collector. Those who remember the old system said that if the teacher got to a word he did not understand he called it a 'passover'. Often the school would be a private house, or maybe just a room in that house, with an earth floor and one end occupied by the teacher's dog or a few chickens. Even in the sixteenth and seventeenth centuries there were schools of a sort, though it was a case of 'no pay, no education'.

There were some queer characters presiding over some of the nineteenth century schools. There was one such who ran a fee-paying school in Long Riston in 1845. He was a strict disciplinarian and had some peculiar ways of punishing his pupils. One was to chalk the shape of a grave on the mud floor of the schoolroom and a boy who had played truant had to strip off his clothes and was then told he was going to be buried alive. One scholar was then sent for a pick and shovel.

By now the erring boy was in a state of panic and the master asked if he would do it again. The lad was now glad to promise anything and was never absent again. As this was the only school for miles around, when the parents objected they were told they could take their children elsewhere. Even so, he is said to have turned out pupils proficient in the '3Rs'.

He got the pupils to collect money from their parents for a trip to the seaside, then said the money was insufficient and should be spent on a telescope, though with a proviso that the pupils could look through it from Monday to Friday. They had one look through and never saw it again, as the schoolmaster used it for his hobby of astronomy.

In the early nineteenth century Hornsea, with 133 families, had no schools. Hutton Cranswick, with 148 families,, had three. Of course, this would not mean that the children of Hornsea were completely untaught. There would be part-time teachers who would impart knowledge in the room of a house, which would not be recognised as a school.

There are still quite a few people who remember the school in Hutton Road, or rather the remains of it. When I went to school just before and during the First World War, there was only one wall of the building still standing. This was at the northern end of a garden of about quarter of an acre occupied by Mr Nendick of the Cross Keys. This was sold by the Education Authority in 1908 and when the first council houses were built in 1925, the garden and school site were taken in with the grass verge of the highway. Mr. Arthur Potter, who with his family farmed Whinnyforth farm for sixty years, remembers swinging on the doors of the school as a child. It was a little building with half doors and was partially demolished soon after. Arthur's father was a pupil at that school and typical of that time. The schoolmaster, a Mr Richardson, was also a shopkeeper.

The pupils paid either 4d. or 6d. a week and, as mentioned before, it was a case of 'no pay, no education'. The old school in Hutton Road is marked on the 1850 map as the 'Parochial School', but on the Enclosure Map there is nothing at all.

At one of these nineteenth century schools near Hull, the teacher, who was also the rate collector, was going to decamp with the rate money and an eighteen-year-old pupil teacher. So life was not all together dull. The children were often absen,. birdscaring, harvesting and doing other seasonal jobs. At ten most of them left school for ever.

Children were often employed singling turnips or mangolds, when the father or some other adult had some turnips to hoe 'bi takl.' That meant contracting to hoe and single roots at so much an acre. Whoever was doing the hoeing could get on much faster if someone was pulling out the bunches and the double plants. They could also earn quite a bit more money. The child would get a few coppers a day; but if he was working for father he would probably get nothing.

The Infants' School, now the Church Rooms, was built in 1844. The following is an extract from a document in the archives at Beverley:

> By donations given by the following landowners in the parish, together with grants from the National Society for the Education of the Poor, in the principals of the established church, and from the Committee of Council on Education. The total cost including the conveyance of the ground and enrolling

and registering the grant, furniture of the school, and materials for enclosing and levelling the grounds amounts to £240.5s.0d. The document goes on to say:

> The levelling of the ground, setting of the posts and rails to enclose it, the leading for the building were done at the expense of the parish and by individual farmers.

The school and the grounds were conveyed to Trustees and it was to be used for a school for children of poor persons in the parish. The education was to be given in connection with the National Society in the Principles of the Established Church and under the supervision of the Lord of the Manor, Lord Hotham, with the church wardens. The schoolmaster or mistress also had to be a member of the church. Here is a list of subscribers:

Lord Hotham gave the land from off the green and donated	£35.0.0d
Edward Horner Reynard, Sunderlandwick	£21.0.0d
William Dennison, landowner	£10.0.0d
Marmaduke Langley, landowner	£10.0.0d
George Hudson, landowner	£ 2.0.0d
Richard Bethell, landowner	£ 2.0.0d
Richard Boyle, landowner	£10.0.0d
Richard Jennings	£10.0.0d
The National Society for the Education of the Poor	£50.0.0d

(Richard Jennings was also the Secretary)

The Jennings were solicitors in Driffield for about a hundred years. I believe the last one was William. Jennings, coroner and Magistrate's Clerk at the beginning of this century, and was still Magistrate's Clerk in the early 1920s.

The Infant School Certificate 1845

> We the undersigned, being desirous of connecting the Infants' School for the benefit of the poor at Hutton Cranswick in the county of York with the National Society, do hereby certify that the education in such school is to be conducted in the principles of the established church and by masters or mistresses who are members of the same and we further declare that we shall be

ready to report upon the state and progress of the school from time to time.

Signed by: E.H. Reynard
R. Jennings
R. Dove
J. Rigby
F. Jennison
J. Grainger
C. Jennings

R.Dove was a shopkeeper as well as church warden and lived in Cranswick; J. Rigby as the vicar; F. Jennison was a shopkeeper; and J. Grainger farmed Scurf Dyke. E.H. Reynard lived at Sunderlandwick Hall.

In 1927 the school was claimed by the church, and this caused quite a bit of resentment in the village, as the parishioners thought that, as their forebears had contributed most to the building, it should have been the property of the parish. On the basis of the facts, the parishioners would seem to have a cast-iron case, but apparently the school's certificate connecting the school with the National Society gave the church the title and the little school is now the Church Rooms. I do not think the church would be able to claim any building today under the same circumstances.

With the Education Acts of 1870 and 1899, together with a later Act in 1902, the power of the church in schools was greatly reduced. Even so, I remember a friend of mine applying for the headship of a school on the Wolds. This was during the last war and direction of labour was very much in force. He did not want the job particularly, but had to go and look round the school. The interviewer asked if he was a member of the Church of England, as this was supposed to be an essential qualification, and he replied that hedid not mind what he belonged to, whether it was the Salvation Army or anything else. To his relief hedid not get the job.

CHAPTER SEVENTEEN

EDUCATION ACT 1870 AND ONWARDS

School Days

After the passing of the Act and compulsory state education for all, whatever their circumstances, things began to move, and the old system of semi-literate part time teachers, with their 4d. a week pupils, were consigned to the limbo of forgotten things. Though there was often opposition to any advance in education, as it was often thought, the bigger the blockhead, the better the worker. That attitude persisted well into this present century. The Hutton Cranswick Primary School was built in 1875 by Charles Watson of Hutton. The cost of the school with house included was £800, and lately it has been enlarged considerably. What the price would be for building it today would be anyone's guess. The school was established under these terms:

> Regulations for the management of Hutton Cranswick Board School 1872:
>
> No religious catechism or formulary which is distinctive of any particular denomination shall be taught in the school.
>
> A portion of the Holy Scriptures shall be read daily by the Headmaster of the School, immediately on its assembly, at nine o'clock in the morning, such reading to continue not more than 15 minutes, but any scholar may be withdrawn by his parent from such reading.
>
> The following to be the essential subjects of Instruction: Reading, Writing and Arithmetic; English Grammar and Composition; The Principles of Bookkeeping; The History of England; Elementary Geography; Elementary Drawing; Singing and Drill
>
> The weekly fees shall be 2d for each of the children of the labouring class and 3d for all others, payable in advance.
>
> First School Board 1872-75:
> E.H. Reynard, Esq.   Chairman
> William Parker.   Farmer
> William Barker.   Grocer

Robert Hardy.	Farmer
John Hobson Wardell. Hutton.	Mole Killer

Second School Board 1875:

William Barker. Hutton.	Grocer
Jonathan Dunn. Cranswick.	Farmer
William Jackson. Hutton.	Farmer
John H. Wardell. Hutton.	Mole Killer
Two vacancies	

The other members of the first Board often had disagreements with E.H. Reynard, which may have been the reason why he was not on the 1875 Board. John Hobson Wardell lived in Front Street, Hutton, opposite the blacksmith's shop. Two bungalows now stand on the site of his house. He died in 1919.

The children from the age of five to seven went to the little Infant School, now the Church Rooms, where there was a headmistress and a pupil teacher. They then graduated to the larger school, where they remained until they were fourteen. The first schoolmaster at the senior school was Mr Rayner, who I can remember living in retirement in a little house on Hutton Road.

Here is a tale from the early years of that school told to me by a relative. The schoolmaster, Mr Rayner, in a pompous manner, said to one of the boys: 'What are you going to be when you grow up, my boy?' Quick as a flash the boy replied, 'A shitlinger, sir'. 'Come out you vulgar brute,' said the teacher and the miscreant was duly whacked. The boy had got this from some of the farm lads and thought he was showing his superior knowledge. This term was usually applied to a lad,'fost year off' (first year hired) as it was called, one who had just left school and milked the house cow as well as feeding the pigs and bullocks. They were also sometimes called 'clagger' or 'trigger'. Some of these were also older men who had a physical or sometimes mental disability, and were looked down on by those who worked with horses. The chap who now milks the cows and 'does' the bullocks has the grandiose title of herdsman.

In those days before the First World War, conditions were totally different both schoolwise or any other wise from those of today. The average wage of most of the parents of the schoolchildren would be about 15s. to £1 a week, whether wage-earners or self-employed.

If we look back to the Parish Magazine of 1909 we can see that nobody was exactly rolling in wealth, it would be just before the First World War that two boys of one family left school early each Wednesday at noon to collect soup from Cattons of South Hall. Pocket money was non-existent and anything extra in the way of a few coppers had to be earned. There was sometimes an opportunity to earn a few coppers a day pulling brassocks. As the working day usually lasted from seven in the morning until five at night, and it often meant getting up before 6 o' clock, most of the lads decided it was not worth it. That was long before the days of spraying.

All children living less than three miles away had to walk and were expected to be on time whatever the weather. None of the children possessed bikes until they left school and earned enough to buy one. Those from Watton Carr and Rotsea were taken to the school in horse buses, and brought their dinners with them. They ate them in the school porch, classrooms, or anywhere they could, and nobody bothered much about what happened to them. There were no vacuum flasks then, and I can't remember anyone bringing round pots of tea.

There were no trips in school hours, educational or otherwise. You might be let out to carry the schoolmaster's coals in when they were tipped out at his gate. This was a bit of free labour, and I wonder how he would have reacted if any of his pupils had refused. Of course, in those days such a thing was unheard of.

The big event of the school year was the annual trip to Bridlington, or Bollington as it was called in the local dialect. All scholars got the fare paid from Cranswick Station and also 6d to spend. That was a day to look forward to, a red letter day; though sometimes the weather turned nasty and a great part of the day was spent sheltering in the railway station.

Two other special days for schoolchildren were Christmas Day and New Year's Day. The boys went round the houses on Christmas Day morning as early as possible and shouted:

> Mistress and Maister,
> Hoo di ya doo,
> A good fat pig and a new cauved coo,
> If ya ain't gor a sixpence,
> Then a halfpenny will do,
> If ya ain't gor a halfpenny,
> Then God bless you.
> Please willya gimmi a Christmas Box?

The line 'If ya ain't gor a halfpenny then God bless you' was sometimes omitted as some crusty individuals took it as a personal insult.

The first boy at a house was the 'lucky bod'. He was supposed to get a silver coin. It was never more than sixpence and they were very few and far between. Yet to a child of that time it was a huge sum. Often one of the older boys of a family had to take one or more of his small brothers along to get them initiated into the 'serious business' of Christmas Boxing. This involved a sharing of the proceeds which big brother didn't like. He could get on much faster himself and the small ones sometimes made a mess of things by shouting 'Mistress and Maistress', or something equally silly. The parents would bully the big lad into taking the younger ones with him. He got his own back by cuffing the ears of some of his charges. When Christmas Day came round again he may have been 'hired off' and the young ones would be taking someone still younger Christmas Boxing.

The most from one household was often a penny and an orange. The total might add up to two or three shillings, sometimes less.

Girls were not supposed to go on Christmas Day. An odd one or two sometimes did and were told they would get nothing. New Year's Day was their day. An elder sister sometimes took a small brother Christmas Boxing, but she kept out of sight when the door of the house opened. When the girls went New Year's Gifting their message was:

> Mistress and Maister,
>
> Happy New Year,
> Please will ya gimmi a New Year's Gift?

There were unwritten rules which were strictly adhered to. No children visited any houses except on Christmas Day for the boys and New Year's Day for the girls. If they had called at any other time they would have been told to come on the proper day. No-one knows how long Christmas Boxing and New Year's Gifting has gone on. It may have been for centuries. In Hutton Cranswick it lasted until just before the Second World War, though it was declining long before that.

Like most schools of that time, there were no sports facilities (that was to come later, after the First World War). Cricket was usually played with a soft ball, with a stake from the hedge as a bat, and a coat as a wicket. Very rarely there might be a boy who had a bat, or maybe a set of wickets. Though if he got out he often departed in a huff and took his bat or wickets with him; that meant the end of the game.

Football was usually played with any ball that was handy and a pair of coats at either end substituted for goal posts. I can't think of any of the bigger boys who went to school in anything else but hobnailed boots. They were usually made by the local cobbler and made to last. There was also a Mr Hensby from Wansford, a kind of itinerant cobbler, who used to come round with footwear.

Shoes were for cissies, and those boots built like battleships were just the thing for playing football. When picking a side you usually tried to get those with the biggest feet and boots. When tackling an opponent the tactics were to kick his shins first, and having made him retire partially crippled, you might score a goal. Crude, but effective.

The clothes worn by most of the pupils were usually fustian or corduroy, and like the boots, they were made to last. In fact some of those corduroys had gone to school for years, as they were often handed down from the eldest of a family, and as they outgrew them they were donned by the younger members.

There was then no dry cleaning and when some offender was beaten by the school teacher, clouds of dust used to rise. It was almost like beating a rug. These corduroys and fustians had an aroma of their own and a shower of rain used to make it more noticeable.

Boot inspection was an essential part of morning school. The scholars were lined up near the entrance, like soldiers on parade, and those whose boots were not up to the required standard were punished. As one boy had to plough until his father came to relieve him just before school, he was always in trouble.

The East Yorkshire dialect, 'broad Yorkshire' as it was usually called then, was beyond the pale and was not allowed to be used in school under any circumstances. I think most of the scholars got to be bilingual, as it were, and kept the 'broad Yorkshire' to be used outside school hours. Most of the teachers seemed to think it was the language of an uncouth ignoramus and anyone using it was punished accordingly. They seemed to forget, or maybe did not know, that the children were speaking the tongue of their forefathers from over the North Sea, the Danes, Vikings, Norsemen, or whoever made up those marauding parties who visited this coast over a thousand years ago and left so much of their language as a legacy.

In those days, before radio, television, etc., began to bombard the public with what they called 'standard English', most of the parents spoke in the vernacular and the children, as was to be expected, did the same. Though nowadays the East Yorkshire dialect has lost its uncouth image probably this is in some way due to the late Austin Hyde and the Yorkshire Dialect Society - it is fast disappearing. Suburban educational methods and teachers who know little about it have seen to that. I wonder what would be the reaction of today's teachers, especially those brought up in a town, if some of their pupils addressed them in pure unadulterated dialect. They would wonder what on earth they were saying and act in the same way as their predecessors of over sixty years ago.

From 'broad Yorkshire' back to the old school in the Edwardian and early Georgian days. Most of the children disliked school. To go further, I think many of them, positively hated it. The teachers in the main did their job well, and they stood no nonsense. They were there to impart education and that is just what they did, though sometimes it seemed as though they were hammering nails in a piece of wood. The teachers may have often thought the same thing. There was never any question of making the teaching or the curriculum more attractive to the pupils. In fact, to most of them education was like taking a nasty dose of medicine, something which had to be endured.

Today we often hear of there being a certain percentage of illiterate pupils leaving school at sixteen, and even the same thing among university entrants. I cannot remember anyone who left school during the period and just after the First World War who was in that class. If the old schoolmaster thought any of his pupils were not going to quit themselves creditably in that direction he would have had the hide off him.

As I said before, the teachers stood no nonsense and soon used the cane to enforce discipline. There were various ideas thought up by the scholars, to ameliorate the effects of a caning. One was to rub onion on the hands so that the cane would slip off but as nobody knew what part of the anatomy was going to be attacked, this ruse never worked. You were always the loser.

Some of the women were as adept with the cane as the men, and they took mixed classes as well. One old battle-axe could use a pointer, as we called it, like any one of the Three Musketeers could wield a sword. These pointers may still be used today. Then it was a polished stick about four feet long, strongly made and tapered slightly. You could have felled an adult with it. They were used for pointing things out on the blackboard, and the teacher could stand well back and not obscure the scholar's view.

This same teacher (I can't remember her name) was usually armed with this thing and advance on an offending pupil with it raised in the air. He shot under the desk for protection but was brought to the surface with a shrewd dig in the ribs. She then beat him down again. What a row there would be if such a thing happened today. Even then the teachers were often threatened by angry parents, though I don't think it ever got to physical violence.

Perhaps those teachers of all those years ago may have 'builded better than they knew' and gave some of the children a taste for books and literature which lasted a lifetime, though in many homes at that time you would hardly find even a newspaper for reading, and the local newspaper was about the only source of information available. I remember hearing a story from my mother (this would be long before the days of radio) of an old lady living in one of the Wold villages who told her neighbours of some happening or other. The neighbour did not believe her so the old lady said 'A coarse its right, Ah saw it in Thriffield Tarms'. An implicit faith in the press.

As most of the parents at that time worked from six to six and six days a week until the First World War, there wasn't much time for reading, even if they had had the inclination. After working hard all day, they wouldn't feel very intellectual, though in quite a few homes you would find well-thumbed copies of the classics. The County libraries did not come into being until the early 1920s and were a great boon to the villagers. Since then we have got evening classes of every description catering for all age groups.

The outlook for those approaching schoolleaving age in the early part of this century was very limited Even in the years before the Second World War, it wasn't much better, though the huge unemployment figures must be taken into account. There were a few scholarships, but most of the parents could not afford to keep a child who would not be earning anything for a while, so a bright child had little opportunity for further advancement and not many continued with schooling after the age of fourteen. A few, and a very few, went on to be teachers.

At that time there was not the vast army of minor bureaucrats, local government officials, etc., all non-productive, who abound today. All these require clerks, typists and form-fillers to assist them. Neither were there the agricultural colleges, now spread over the country, running residential and part-time courses, in which school-leavers and pre-school-leavers can participate. Indeed, agriculture, like the East Yorkshire dialect, was considered to be uncouth and dirty, and schoolchildren were encouraged to get as far away from it as possible.

I remember the schoolmaster giving some of the older boys a long harangue and telling them: 'You don't want to go on to farms, you want to get something better'. He had a captive audience and no one could ever answer back. Most of them wondered what it was all about, particularly as he never told them what sort of job they should get, and as an educationalist he should have known something about the position, especially the economic one. Apart from these tirades, which to the listening pupils seemed an exercise in futility, I don't think he bothered his head much.

So, most of the scholars left school at fourteen, went on to farms as wag lads or 'thoddy lads' and left their education behind forever. Most of the girls went into domestic service for a few shillings a week, 'lived in', and worked unlimited hours. 'Fost year off' was a rough life for a lad, but most of them were glad to see the last of school.

During the First World War, quite a few were allowed to leave school at thirteen, provided they passed what was called the Labour Exam. Some were allowed to leave school without taking it, as food production was considered to be more important than a child's education, and to the lads it was a heaven-sent opportunity to get away from the tyranny of school. Those whose fathers were tradesmen or craftsmen often followed their fathers into the business, that is if there weren't too many of them. Then some of them usually ended up on the land. In those days the old adage 'pulling yourself up by your bootlaces' certainly applied.

No mention of the Edwardian and Georgian school days would be complete without Miss Bracey. The daughter of a Congregational Minister originally from Norfolk, she served the school and the village for about half a century. When she started teaching is obscure, as some of the earlier school records were destroyed. A feminine counterpart of Mr Chips, she retired in 1938, came back during the war years and finally gave up teaching at the end of hostilities. Even then she did not sever all connections with the school, but was always willing to help the school and scholars in any capacity. She will always be remembered with respect and affection by those she taught during fifty years at Cranswick school. She died at Driffield a few years ago aged 91.

In the years between the wars, conditions in the schools improved to a certain extent. S.E.J. Best, in his book *East Yorkshire,* 1930, expressed the view that a central school ought to be erected to accommodate the children of eleven plus years from the surrounding five or six villages, where they would receive a more efficient teaching than they would in a small country school. He then goes on to say that this would put the burden of transport on to the County Council, and the expense to the parents of providing meals, even if only sandwiches out of a very small wage. The wages of most of the parents of the children at that time was 32s. a week.

Best must have had second sight, though he could hardly have envisaged the Welfare State with child allowances, canteens and transport provided. When the Second World War was over, education had vast amounts of money spent on it with the building of new schools and universities. Whether it has been value for money is another matter. Now education is facing severe economy cuts.

CHAPTER EIGHTEEN

COWS, PIGS AND PONDS

Dr W. Wood of Middleton-on-the-Wolds was Medical Officer for health at the beginning of this century. His districts were Hutton Cranswick and Middleton. He was instrumental in getting two ponds filled up at Hutton as a danger to health. One was in Front Street near the telephone box and close to where the village pump stood. The other was at the bottom of Church Lane where it meets Mill Street.

This must have caused a great deal of hardship to the village people, especially the cottagers, many of whom kept a cow, as when there was no rain all the water had to be pumped. That meant a lot of hard work, as the wells in Hutton were very deep, though they never went dry.

Everybody was careful to conserve all the water and tubs were always kept underneath the fall pipes of houses and buildings. These were mostly wood and were hooped. Some had been cattle treacle containers and after a spell of dry weather they would leak like a sieve until the wood swelled sufficiently to hold water.

The nearest stream, Skerne Beck, or Northfield Beck as the stretch nearest Hutton is called, is half a mile away at its nearest point. At its farthest it will be nearly a mile. In a dry summer the stock owner had sometimes to take a cart or rully loaded with barrels, milk cans, or anything which would hold water, and fill them up there. Those nearest Cranswick went to the pond in the Main Street. All this took up a great deal of time, especially during harvest when labour was needed elsewhere. Even so, this was easier than the endless pumping.

In the days before piped water, the ponds were invaluable, whether they were field ponds or village ponds. Those old dewponds on the Wolds are a good example. Piped water was brought to the village just before the Second World War, when the Southburn Road pumping station was built, and made life a lot easier for the villagers. Though electricity had arrived eight years earlier, many villagers would rather have had the water first.

Incidentally, when the project was first discussed at a meeting in the Foresters Hall in 1935, the schoolmaster was one of those who opposed it. Having got the water he said the sewerage would be sure to follow. Not a very enlightened view, as I believe he was also a Rural District Councillor.

Many houses did not possess a well or pump. In Mill Street there was one pump for nine houses, and it was situated at the end one. Chalk Pit Cottages had every drop of water to carry from the parish pump in Front

101

Street, a distance both ways of over a quarter of a mile, apart from what could be collected from the roofs. This old pump was removed not so many years ago.

When a pump bucket began to wear, the local blacksmith had to re-leather it, and I can remember having one done for the last time in 1938. This meant getting a ladder, sometimes two fastened together, and going down the well. This was dry, though dark at the bottom, but with the light of a candle the old craftsman made a good job. It was essential not to drop any pebbles down from the top as you might hear a howl and a few swear words from the bottom. Many of those deep wells are still there, some only covered by a flagstone and a thin layer of earth. One has a garden path over it, and there is said to be a bag of workman's tools at the bottom. One houseowner decided to fill in his well which was in the kitchen, and his mother was horrified to find she had been standing on some not very safe boards over it doing the washing for over thirty years.

There is now renewed interest in these old wells and many are now being preserved. However, those who lost so much sweat swinging these 'one armed Charlies', as they were sometimes called, were glad to see them go.

How the old Doctor got away with filling the ponds in we shall never know, as most of the villagers of that generation were fiercely independent and would not be pushed around by anyone. It is also surprising that the one at Cranswick was left untouched. After all, the bottom half of Cranswick was, and still is, well supplied by natural springs.

Some of the ponds used to get a bit filthy in summer, sometimes they were like mud holes. But water is the lifeblood of a community and it did not matter so long as it was wet and the stock could be satisfied. But in 1933 when the Milk Marketing Board took over the control of the milk trade, they looked on the ponds with disfavour, and many of them in the fields were filled in when mains water arrived.

It is always the easiest way to take stock to the water than the other way round. Thus the two ponds in Hutton would be handy for the adjacent owners of stock. The lane cows would get a drink as they came by morning and evening. The same would apply to Cranswick.

From time immemorial the cottagers' cows will have grazed the lanes and, before the Enclosures, the commons as well. Even in the 1920s and early 1930s the lanes were let by the Parish Council. There were usually about forty cows and a cow 'gate' cost the owner 3s. each. The cows from Hutton and those from Cranswick were kept separate and a cow 'tenter' appointed for each village. The cow tenter's wage was 9s. per week. It was a strict rule that each cow should be hutted; that meant wrapping the end of its horns with tightly-woven twine and tar. This blunted the animal's horns and lessened the risk of them injuring one another. There was then no dehorning and a number of strange cows together usually meant fights until they settled down. At one lane letting a subcommittee was appointed to see that all animals were hutted. As the 'thirties advanced the lane cows disappeared, due in part to the agricultural depression when hay and grass eatage were practically given away, and to the fact that the villager was better off than before the First World War. The lanes were grazed by local farmers during the Second World War and supervised by a cow tenter. When the war was over the lane letting ended.

Many of the cottagers also kept a pig or two as well as a cow. There was often a small paddock attached to the house and some still have a little building or two where a cow or pig could be housed. The paddock would supply hay for the winter, and the cow would graze the lanes in summer along with the others.

The pigs would live on household scraps and corn gleaned by the children from the harvest field. Until the binder came on the scene there was quite a lot of loose corn left behind, and this with small potatoes would often keep a pig the year round until his demise as a baconer. Nothing can ever equal the taste of pig taties boiled in their skins and eaten just before they got to the pigs. A bit of muck seemed to give them an added flavour.

The cream was made into butter and sold to the local shopkeeper, or maybe a huckster who would sell it at the nearest market. Making butter could be an aggravating process, especially if it refused to 'turn', that is, it just remained sloppy. It was sometimes said that to put half-a-crown in the churn would do the trick. That was more of a joke than anything else. I remember one man who., after watching his wife turning the churn for hours and getting no results, saying 'Ah got auld bloody lot, an threw it id pig swill tub. It maird dord pigs' tails coll'.

In dry summers I often heard people say how they wished the Beck with its clear spring water could be moved near the village. The answer would have been to have laid a system of pipes from the springs feeding the streams and pumped it up to the houses. Of course, it was never as simple as that. Right up to the early 1930s very few local authorities were prepared to spend money on a village, even though labour was cheap and a lot of hard work only realised 9d an hour. Even today when rural and urban areas pay the same rates, the country seems to be the last to benefit.

Now we are sometimes threatened with a water shortage, and not so long ago there were cut-offs and a kind of rationing by putting stand pipes in the streets, with banning of the use of hosepipes. Yet a tremendous amount of water is wasted. What we used to conserve so carefully in tubs and barrels now just runs off the houses and down the drains.

Nearly all the houses on the Wolds had no other water supply except from cisterns supplied from the roofs and which was used for everything. The nearest fresh water supply was often miles away.

Anyone who has recently come to live in one of the older houses in the parish may often wonder why the soil in his garden is so friable. This is the result of a hundred years or more of ashes from the privy being spread on it. The ashes, from the kitchen grate, were to neutralise the stink. In a town it was called night soil, and truck loads of it were sent to village stations where it was picked up by farmers and spread on the land. It was also available in Driffield where it was practically given away. Often it was used for drilling with turnips, was a cheap form of 'manishment' (fertiliser), and seemed to give good results. That was before the days of compound fertilisers. In a town it was collected by the urban authorities, whereas in a village the onus was on the householder. Thus an occupier often had nowhere to dump it except the garden.

Sometimes it was a case of backing a cart up to the privy and 'mucking out' every two or three months. These old shacks were often made of wood and were given some unflattering names. They usually stood as far away from the house as possible: rather inconvenient in certain circumstances. I can remember one farm where it was about a hundred yards from the house. Often they would hide modestly behind a lilac tree or a few creepers, and how those blossoms flourished. Ivor Novello must have been thinking of those marvellous blooms when he wrote 'We'll Gather Lilacs'.

I can remember one occasion when the driver of a tipping lorry was delivering a load of gravel to a house in Cranswick. He had taken the load a hundred yards or so behind the house and when returning empty had forgotten that the vehicle body was still up. A clothes line was stretched from an old lavatory to a tree and the lorry body caught the line and brought the whole lot down. What with the occupier's bad language and the resultant pong, the air was quite blue.

The sewerage system came to Cranswick in 1961 and Hutton in 1974, and so at last we are supplied with all mod. cons. etc. Due to distance, most of the outlying parts of the parish are not connected to the drainage system, yet on the creation of the new local authorities a few years ago, all these rate-payers were charged for non-existent services, in that they were rated the same as those directly connected to the sewers. Later, after considerable pressure, reason prevailed, and those who had paid sewerage charges had a refund and that part of the rating system amended in their favour.

From the Parish Council Minutes

December 1907: J. Emsley was paid £1.10s.0d for nine days work carting sludge from Cranswick pond. That would be for himself and a horse and cart. Tom Dixon and George Green were also paid £1.11s.6d. each for nine days work which is about 3s.5 ½ d. a day. They had to fill the carts with 'dirt as the Council Clerk put it. This was hard manual labour; even so, they were better off than their neighbours engaged in agriculture, who at that time were working 65 hours a week for 15s., as the pond diggers would be working an hour or two less a day than the farm worker. That applied to drainers, dyke cleaners, etc., then and for a long time after.

January 1908: The Council decided that application should be made to the Earl of Londesborough and Lord Hotham to supply land for allotments. At the next meeting on the 30th of the same month the Committee appointed to confer with Mr Armstrong (Reynard's steward) had reported that Mr F. Reynard had decided to withdraw the Common Fields from the occupation of the Council at the expiration of the lease. He offered a renewal of the lease of the Megginson fields at an increased rent of 3s. an acre. At the same meeting it was decided that the Council were strongly opposed to a renewal of the lease at an increased rent. The Clerk was instructed to write to Mr Reynard setting out the objections to the curtailment of the lease and increased rents. A letter was produced from Mr O'Callaghan, the vicar, to a member of the Council in which he expressed the willingness of Mr Reynard to renew the lease on the present terms. A copy of this letter was to be enclosed.

At the next meeting, on 11 February, the tenants were to be asked by a vote to state whether they would retain the land on the terms offered by Mr Reynard. In the Minutes it says: 'The motion was supported by five of the tenants and rejected by a large majority of them'. Later, at the same meeting, it was decided that as a majority of the tenants did not wish to retain their land at an increased rent, Mr Reynard's offer was declined. The Council would buy the land from Mr Reynard if he wished to sell, and the Earl of Londesborough and Lord Hotham were to be asked again if they could sell or let land to the Council. Mr F. Reynard, 'Auld Freddy', was a 'hard backedun' whose motto seemed to be 'If thoo dis owt fur nowt, dea it fur thissen'.

April 8th, 1908: The East Riding County Council was to be asked to help in obtaining land and a large number of rate payers urged the Council to obtain land before April 1908. Nowadays, when much of the Parish Council's work is giving its views on planning, which are often ignored, where or not to build houses, and food is expected to appear automatically in the shops or supermarkets, obtaining land to grow food seems to our increasingly urbanised society to be a relic of the past. At that period of the twentieth century, though the Old Age Pension of 5s. a week had just begun, land and food were essential, and those ratepayers knew that if they did not help themselves nobody else would.

15 January 1909: A letter was received from Mr T. Holtby, Solicitor, Driffield, containing an offer made by Mr Mark Sykes, Sledmere, to lease a farm to the Council for the term of fourteen years at a rental of £145 per annum. The Council had the option to purchase during the lease for the sum of £3,100 the farm house at Hutton known as the Manor House, two cottages and land amounting to 158 acres, 3 roods, 1 perch. All but two of the Council voted in favour of accepting the offer. This farm had been sold the preceding August along with other lands belonging to the Hotham estate and was bought by Mark Sykes. At last the villagers' fears of being landless vanished and Mr George Rayner, retired schoolmaster, measured the land as required, though he must have got in a bit of a muddle as one field has 'gairings' at both sides. This I have never seen in a field before. Gairings occur where one end of a field is longer than the other, and this when ploughing or harrowing can cause a lot of time-wasting doing short turns. 'Gairings' is said to be derived from the Icelandic lgejr', an arrowhead. Incidentally the Parish Council had this field and part of another one drained and a Minute of 4 December 1912 reads:

> Thomas Barmby's tender for cutting drains in the allotment fields was accepted. 2 foot deep ls.6d. per chain (22 yards). 3 foot 2s.6d.

Presumably this would include putting in the pipes and filling in after. If Thomas Barmby was living today his tender would, in all probability, be over a hundred times that figure.

30 April 1919: The Parish Council sent a letter to the Clerk of the County Council regarding the buying of the allotment farm and a committee was appointed to take such action as was thought necessary towards that end.

12 November 1919: After receiving a deputation from the Parish Council the previous May the County Council gave their consent to the

purchase of all the land in the occupation of the Parish Council. Application was to be made to the Ministry of Health for permission to borrow money to finance the deal, and the representatives of the late Sir Mark Sykes were to be informed that the Council would buy the farm. (Sir Mark Sykes had died while attending the Peace Conference in Paris.) The transaction was to be completed by April 1921.

On 23 October 1913 the Hutton Cranswick Cricket Club asked the Parish Council for permission to relay and fence in 40 square yards of the green for a cricket and tennis ground. This was granted.

Walter Simpson's brother from Bridlington was in charge of the levelling, etc., at a cost of £40. Walter was a Cranswick tailor. When he began to cut the turf he found it so good that he wished to take it to Headingley cricket ground. He would do all the work for nothing, including returfing, if the club committee would give him permission. However, the cricket club decided against this. The original turf was replaced and when completed the pitch was said to be one of the best in East Yorkshire.

All the heavy work was done by voluntary labour, supervised by Walter Simpson, Alfred Voase, Bustard Nest, and Joe Elsworth, Little Common. Most of this work would be done during the evenings as the Saturday half day for farm workers was still a few years away and Sunday work at that time was very much out of the question.

In 1919 when the war was over and the five-and-a-halfday week was established, the cricket club fulfilled many fixtures with the surrounding villages. Their transport was usually the late W. Wilson's horse bus.

At one of those post-war matches, Arthur Consitt, of Cranswick Grange, was wicket-keeper. He said to one of the fielders: 'When you throw a ball in, throw it straight for my nose end'. Not long after the same fielder threw a ball in with considerable force, Arthur missed it, and was knocked out. When he came round he admitted he couldn't blame the man who threw the ball as he had done exactly as instructed.

Some of those who played in the cricket team just after the war were:

J. Elsworth	H. Milner
A. Voase	F. Gospel
A. Consitt	J. Eccles
S. Duke	R. Wilson
W. Duke	J. Duke

At the same time the Soccer Club was formed. The team's ground was on the old Show Field at the bottom of Southgate. Like many other East Riding villages the club joined the newly-formed Driffield and District League and is still going strong. A friend informs me that he remembers seeing a photograph of a rugby team which played in the field behind the White Horse. That must have been quite a while before the 1914-18 war.

No tennis court was laid out on the green and a few years after the cricket club was formed, a tennis club was created and a court made on a piece of ground in Hutton Road, bought from Mr Acey.

17 November 1920: The allotment farm: having got permission from the Ministry of Health, the Council decided to apply to the Public Works Loan Board for a loan of £2,200 to be repaid in fifty years' time. The following January it was decided to increase the allotment rents by 6s. per acre. The tenants having already given their approval. This would be their contribution towards the financing of the scheme. The Council were not letting grass grow under anyone's feet and three days later the Committee appointed to deal with buying the land were given authority to issue Bonds, or otherwise to raise the required money. By March 1921 the Council had received applications for the 6% Land Bonds to be issued by the Council.

Those who applied were the Hutton Cranswick Foresters Society, who wanted £1,000 and were granted £900. Hutton Cranswick Oddfellows Society, £300, and also nine people living in Cranswick who bought Bonds: eight bought £100 worth each and one £200. The Council Clerk was Mr W. Jackson and this (March, 1921) was his last appearance as Clerk. At the same meeting Mr W. Richardson was appointed his successor, The deal, as everyone had hoped, was completed by April 1921, and it was said to be the first time any Parish Council in England had bought a farm of that size.

There were many trials and tribulations, especially during the 'twenties and 'thirties when parts of the land were untenanted and some was let at a low rent to keep it in cultivation. 45 acres were sold in 1941 when everything was at a low ebb in spite of war-time Government promises. At last in 1971 the land was paid off. That land, which originally cost twenty pounds an acre will now be worth over £2,000 and is an asset to the village and parish for all time. Houses and buildings will eventually fall down, but the land always remains.

January 1922: the Clerk reported that Mr Holtby, Solicitor, Driffield, who had handled the negotiations for the Council during the land-buying programme, had been paid £40 on account for his services and the remainder could be paid, interest free, at the Council's convenience.

Parish Council Elections, April 1922
(Cost £9.4s.0d) Returning Officer: W.R. Braithwaite.

There were twenty-four candidates for thirteen seats. Prior to that election there were speeches in the Foresters Hall and one speaker was imported from Driffield, of whom it was said that he would speak for anyone for the price of a pint of beer. The main object of the election was to get one of the Council Members, Walter Turner, removed. Walter had served the parish well for a number of years, but he was a bit of a rebel and too much of a Labour man for some of his colleagues, most of them being Liberal or Conservative. Walter had been born 60 years too soon. Today he might have been a Trade Union leader or maybe a Member of Parliament. He was one of those who could 'talk the hind legs off a donkey', and once had the chance to be trained as a public speaker. He was also a kind of amateur lawyer. The Council, however, had decided that he was too much of a 'stormy petrel' and wanted to get rid of him. Walter polled a fair amount of votes at the election, but not enough to resume his seat. Now we move on to the next Parish Council Election, 1925. Walter tried again and was unsuccessful. Here is his manifesto preceding that election:

HUTTON CRANSWICK PARISH AND
DISTRICT COUNCIL ELECTION
April 6th, 1925

Fellow Parishioners, Friends and others:

For three long lean years you have been dosed with Reform Mixture, sour and simple. How do you like it?

This mixture has been specially patented, prepared and prescribed by a combine known as Bunker's Rookery and Sheepman Dukery and Spookery, with a whole lot of jiggery pokery thrown in by way of ballast and flavouring.
R is Reform Mixture drunk lying down,
Jolly well watered all fears for to drown.
W for Warning Boards braving the storm
Though it ain't goin' to rain no more one-eyed reform.
And what about the green!

Here again the public warning was issued 'Keep off our sacred patch'.

The gaps in the Concert party were filled by the Throstle singing in the Boughs. At the tearful odds of 11 to 2 the Reform Log Roller scented danger, for when candidates definitely withdrew solely and wholly to avoid the expense of a poll, they were over persuaded by the Whispering Twins, after a long vigil, to withdraw their withdrawals, expense did not count only the 'Strangers could be kept outside the Ark'. The Wiseacres in their sacred wigwam did not know the demand for a poll was bad, as five out of the six signing were not present at the Parish Meeting. Thus a dud notice was unwittingly accepted by the Chairman.

> Who called the Poll? I said the Hogman lute Joined by the Rookery flute We must keep the critics oot We called the Poll.

> Mary had a little lamb It came straight down from Hutton It saw these ugly Warning Boards Then turned to frozen mutton. And how about the allotments?

Does reform mean that most land becoming vacant must change hands by Hole and Corner methods? The Allotment Regulations state that all such plots must be advertised 'To Let'. How many times has this regulation been ignored during the last three years?

> Jesse had a pony fat
> That on the Green did dine,
> It saw one staring, glaring board,
> Then fell and broke its spine. And what about the roadmen?

In a very close vote, with the honourable exception of Mr J.C. Duke, every District Councillor from this area voted for Long Time, five and a half hours extra work for nothing. As a District Councillor and Guardian 1 did put up a real fight for economy, though never at the expense of the poor. My successors have seen the Rates always on the Rise. What have they done? Increased the salaries of the Official class. Do you wonder that numerous Parishes have had to be summoned for rates? While officials ride in comfy and beautiful cars the poor Ratepayers trudge along footsore and weary and are offered Rookery Reform Rub Acids that only swell their aching bunions.

> Hey, diddle, diddle,
> The rats rasped the fiddle
> Thirteen puppies all barked at the moon
> The bluetits all twittered to see such fun
> But the crow caawed nine notes out of tune.

The work of the Guardians has been described as partly that of a scavenger and partly that of a doctor. The hard rough work of the world goes on and leaves a trail of ruin. The Guardians have to clear up this human mess. Hopes blighted, lives slowly wasted, love without possibility of fulfilment, and the certainty for hundreds of long lives spent in ceaseless anxiety, and servitude. It is among people moved by such conditions that I have spent a great part of my life. If you wish to give me a wider field for the exercise of my humble abilities, then Vote on Monday for.

Yours faithfully,

WALTER E. TURNER

Printed and published by Horsley and Dawson, Market Place, Driffield.

The 'long time' Walter mentioned which he said was five and a half hours extra (this was weekly) for nothing, was the cause of the farm workers' abortive strike of 1922. Then the farm workers' hours were increased from nine a day to ten. After a year or two they were reduced to nine and a half. This was what they were in 1925. A year or two later they were back to nine. The local authority workers at that time worked the same hours as his agricultural counterpart. Walter says in this year (1925) the Council workers were working nearly three hours a week longer than the men on the land. So we will leave it at that. Here is another of Walter Turner's pre-election pamphlets in which he lambasts one of his opponents, G. Hobson. The date is unknown, but may have been either of the two elections previously referred to:

HOBSON GEORGE out of Boggle Hall by Sheepman.

> A Bluebook Quoter, a roamer from Skerne Dyke to Rotsea Stream. Part owner of that sturdy horse John Fowler. A great believer in Doctor Green for curing the ills of all animals. Has great faith in Do It Yourself, always carries a few 6in. nails and a length of binder twine, repairs carried out expeditiously, sometimes only temporary. Favourite colour - Deep Blue.

John Fowler was the steam engine, which powered the Hobsons threshing set. The Hobsons did contract threshing in the district for over thirty years. Walter Turner's remarks about the rates being always on the rise, while officials ride in comfortable cars have a familiar ring and could apply today, over half a century later. After all his allegations of skull duggery against the Parish Council, Walter did not get a seat, and was never on the Council again. He died in the late 1930s.

7 July 1928: The Council decided to take steps to find out who was rightful owner of the premises on the Green lately used as an infant school. On 17 October the deputation appointed to investigate the ownership of the school reported that they had obtained the deed from the Record Office and that the school was held in trust by the Vicar and Churchwardens for as long as they required it. That was the end of that, though there must have been much heated discussion in the Council Chamber as the Vicar, the Rev. George Storer, had just commenced duty as a Councillor. He was also the one blamed for 'pinching' the school from the Parish, as many village people called it.

Bottom of Main Street.

School children pose for camera, c. 1913. In background is Arthur Dosser holding reins. On the right is bakery van.

Main Street, Cranswick.

Main Street with Pack Horse, c. 1930.

Railway Station, Cranswick, c. 1905.

Railway Station, Cranswick, c. 1905.

Mr. & Mrs. Dickinson, Coal Merchants, Cranswick at Cranswick Station.

Burn Butts, Cranswick.

Cranswick Village Feast, c. 1900.

CHAPTER NINETEEN

THE FIRST THREE DECADES OF THE TWENTIETH CENTURY

Prior to 1914 the parish had altered very little since 1851 and the village was still a self-contained community, though the tradesmen had decreased over the years. In 1911 the population of the parish had dropped to 967, when there were 240 occupied dwellings. The workers in the fields no longer walked to work along the footpaths, nor did they stumble over the dykes in the dark. They rode cycles along the roads lit by an oil or acetylene lamp, though there were still a few who walked. Buying a cycle was a big item out of a wage of fifteen shillings a week, which worked out at about threepence an hour. Conditions, however, were getting slightly better and though sixty odd hours a week were worked, some of the more laborious tasks such as cutting corn with the scythe or cutting it loose with the sail reaper and then gathering it all and tying into sheaves had gone. Instead all corn was now cut by the binder, and the threshing machine had been well established in the nineteenth century. The binder knotter was regarded by most of those who worked in the harvest fields as a marvellous invention because it put an end to so much drudgery. Binding corn by hand was a task nobody liked because it was a slow, laborious business needing hands and arms with a skin like cast iron. More so if there were some sharp thistles, and yet for centuries our ancestors had bound their corn up in this manner.

In 1909 Lloyd George, then Chancellor of the Exchequer, had to find an additional £15,000,000 in taxation. Part of this was for the Old Age Pensions; some of it for increased armaments; so the Chancellor increased Income Tax by twopence, established a super tax, and increased death duties. All this seems insignificant nowadays when a few billions of pounds are just chicken feed. Then, most of the residents of this parish, apart from a few landowners and some of the larger farms, never earned enough to come within the income tax bracket.

With the outbreak of war in 1914 the Government at last began to realise the value of agriculture, and the German submarines taking a big toll of merchant shipping helped to convince the doubters. At last, though controls were brought in, British agriculture began to be more profitable. A lot of grass was also ploughed up, but that was in the later years of the war.

When the German Navy bombarded Scarborough on 16 December 1914, their guns could be clearly heard in Hutton Cranswick and it seemed as though the war was getting very close. Such a bombardment was never attempted on this part of the coast again, though the Zeppelins bombed Hull with loss of life, and once dropped a bomb on Driffield.

As the war dragged on, conscription was brought in and even those engaged in agriculture, if of military age, had to appear before a Tribunal; if an older man could do their work, they were called up for military service. Sometimes tradesmen and others who were of a low military category had to work a certain amount of hours on the land. The Army took the younger and more able-bodied workers from the fields and it became difficult to find anyone able to carry the bags of corn on threshing days. Wheat was always the biggest problem as it was always weighed out at 18 stones to the sack. That problem was overcome by borrowing men, and in one case a contraption of ropes and pulleys was used to hoist the bags into the granary.

If the farmer was getting a little more prosperous, so was his worker, and before the end of the war and for a little while after, his wage was 49s. a week. The old method of working from six in the morning until six at night for six days of the week was discarded. The Saturday half day was adopted and work stopped at midday. Thus in those few years since 1914 more reforms were achieved than in all the previous centuries and it had taken a major war to bring it about. The Women's Land Army was formed, while others went into munitions factories, and probably for the first time in history, domestic servants were scarce. These examples come from the Driffield Times, 1916:

> At the Driffield Hirings wagoners were getting from £36 to £46 a year. Young lads from £20 to £30.

(These would probably be the third lads, fourth lads, wag lads, down to the boy just leaving school at fourteen.)

> Females through the Registry Office. Cooks £20 to £25; Kitchen maids £15 to £19; First year girls £14.

Less than two years later all the wages of the above had been increased considerably.

Before conscription was introduced the Army was very much in evidence at the Hirings, often with a drum and fife band, trying to tempt any likely lads to join their ranks. They sometimes got a few recruits, though that was often the result of too much beer, rather than patriotism. The famous poster of Lord Kitchener with his pointing finger and the words 'Your King and Country need you' looked down from many a wall and building. He had a tragic end in June 1916 when the cruiser 'Hampshire', in which he was going to Russia, was torpedoed in the North Sea. Another war-time poster was one condemning the demon drink as more of a threat to the country than the Germans and the submarines. I remember seeing one in a mill years after the war ended and Kitchener and his call to arms had long since vanished from the hoardings.

The war was very real as the men being called up increased, and the casualty lists grew; every town, village and hamlet suffered and this parish was no exception, as the War Memorial testifies.

Rationing was introduced in the latter stages of the war, though in many ways it is practically impossible to ration the country man. He can always keep a pig or two, often unknown to the authorities, and like his ancestors through the ages, can usually survive. Being brought up to live frugally, the villager of that era could fall back on his own resources. Before 1914, pig killing was a common event in the village as soon as the end of the year approached. There were then no humane killers and the pig was hit over the head with a hammer and its throat cut while unconscious. There was no more cruelty in this, if done by an expert, than in the modern method. The pig was then scraped and cleaned in a tub of boiling water, cut up and salted down. A lot of salt was needed which in time turned to water, and if some of the new arrivals in this district occupying some of the older houses are wondering where the damp patch in a certain part of the house is coming from, it may be that a pig was 'salted' there at some time. The damp patches from the salt seem to last for generations.

When the war was over there was a kind of false prosperity for a while, with a lot of bogus promises from politicians and much talk of a brave new world. This led agriculturalists and others to expand a little. Some spent money they would not have done if they could have foreseen the future and not put their trust in Government promises. Others took larger farms or bought the ones where they were sitting tenants and had a millstone round their necks for the next twenty years. Most of them lived in a state of semi-bankruptcy until the Second World War.

Conditions were not so bad until 1921 when Lloyd George repealed the Corn Production Act. This was a war-time measure whereby subsidies were paid on corn. The Government, realising that there was a great deal of cheap food available from the Empire and other countries abroad, could not resist the temptation to throw agriculture overboard. 'When farming prospers, so does the Nation' is often quoted and there must be a great deal of truth in it, as in this case when farming was sacrificed for cheap imported food, industry also collapsed.

Just for a while the rural worker had a taste of better things, as had his urban counterpart, until the Depression of 1922 when the farm workers' wage dropped to 32s. a week. At this time a few men cycled from this village every morning to work on the docks at Hull and rode back at night, a round trip of forty miles. That was before the days of decasualisation on the docks. One of them said the money was quite good though he did not say exactly how much. It may have been a shilling an hour, and that was threepence an hour more than he would have got on a farm. It can't have done him any harm as he is still living. Now, working on the docks is a closed shop and the dock workers have complete control.

Trade Union leaders and others who remember those days stress the terrible conditions endured by dock workers, miners and other urban workers, who, if they were out of work, could at least draw unemployment relief. They hardly ever mention the fact that the worker on the land received no 'dole' until 1936.

The farm workers strike of 1922 was the aftermath of the Repeal of the Corn Production Act. The younger ones, who were hired by the year, had been engaged at Martinmas (1921) on a fixed contract, though at a greatly reduced rate. In February 1922 they were asked to work an hour a day longer for the same rate of pay, to which they objected. Some ceased work while others carried on. Their protests usually consisted of going round farms where there were employed men working and 'lowsing' the horses out of the ploughs and harrows. As they were on private property, some of them were taken to court and fined. Those married men, especially those in tied cottages, couldn't do much about it and there was hardly any other work to go to. I remember one man who was a Labour supporter inciting his fellow-workers to strike while he still remained at work. His employer didn't like it and gave him his notice. As he was in a tied cottage, he had to move promptly. His family moved in with relatives and he was domiciled in a wash house. After a few weeks the strike collapsed completely.

The hardship was not all on the side of the employee, and I remember one man living in Cranswick who had been a foreman on a medium-sized farm saying that when he left, his employer was completely bankrupt. He had bought plough strings out of his own pocket just to keep his boss going and the only reason for leaving him was because he couldn't pay the men's wages.

In 1925 the Government introduced sugar beet growing into this country and helped with advice from their experts. I believe there was also a small subsidy. Beet was grown on all sorts of land, some of it heavy, wet and unsuitable, but anything where there was a pound or two an acre profit was acceptable. There were then no machines for harvesting the crop. The only method was to go through it with a beet plough to cut the roots, then pull it all by hand, and a dreary, backbreaking job it was too. This usually coincided with wheat sowing and, as the sowing nearly always got preference, the beet pulling was relegated to the dark and wet months of November and December. Thus it began to get unpopular, and at the 1925 Driffield hirings some of the lads were asking their would-be employers if they were growing sugar beet. If they said 'yes', the deal was off.

Hoeing was also a hard and tedious job, as the experts said fifteen or sixteen pounds of seed per acre should be used, and that it was foolish to economise in that direction. They hadn't it to hoe, so they would not bother their heads unduly about improved methods of cutting down the seed rate while at the same time getting a good stand of plants per acre. In the Second World War, sugar beet growing was compulsory and the seed rate was usually cut down to six pounds or less, whatever the Government advisers said. Nowadays hoeing is practically eliminated due to precision sowing and pre-emergence spraying.

The price of sugar beet at the factory kept dropping. In 1933 it was just over £2 a ton at 17 ½ sugar. By 1939 it was not much over 30s. When wartime regulations and allocations were dispensed with, very little beet was grown in this parish and today there is none. It is now a specialised industry using the drier and lighter land. In some ways the sugar beet industry did the country a bit of good, as several new factories were built and the railways carrying the bulk of the raw beet to them had increased traffic during the autumn and winter months. There were then no mechanical beet lifting machines, and if extra pullers were needed they were sent by the Employment Exchange. It didn't matter what trade or profession they had belonged to before signing on, if they refused to go with the beet pulling gangs their 'dole' was immediately cut. Clerks and a variety of mixed trades were sent into the beet fields.

The LNER, as it was then, was facing increasing competition from road haulage, and in one case was taking beet from the farm to Southburn station in their own lorries for nothing, provided the beet grower paid the rail charge to the factory. There may have been many such cases in other parts of the country. Another thing that didn't please some of the growers was the fact that they were paying more for beet pulp (which was just residue) from the factory, than they were receiving for the unprocessed article with all the sugar in it. That was after allowing for the fact that a grower was allowed to have a certain amount of pulp at a cheaper rate based on the tonnage he sent to the factory.

Hutton Cranswick was now becoming less of a self-contained unit, and the local trades were slowly dying out. During the 1920s the village tailors went out of business as cheap mass production firms started turning out all kinds of clothing. A made-to-measure suit could be obtained for fifty shillings. Some were as low as thirty, and as the buses came on the roads, the fare to Hull and back cost only 2s.6d., and the fare between Driffield and this village was 5d. return for many years. It would now be 46p.

For a few years after the war, Mr A. Theaker operated a motor bus between Hutton Cranswick, Driffield, and some of the surrounding villages, until the East Yorkshire Bus Company forced it off the road. There were many villages where an enterprising local resident ran a combined passenger and goods carrying service. Most of these were taken over by a large bus company, who then had the monopoly. Here again, we seem to have gone full circle, as the bus companies, now nationalised, want to get rid of all the rural routes. At the moment many of them are being subsidised by the local authority and it is often proposed that a small bus should ply between villages and the nearest town, just like the dual-purpose vehicle of fifty-five years ago.

There was one attempt to break the monopoly of the East Yorkshire Bus Company in the late 1920s, when the Driffield and District Motor Bus Company was formed. It ran between Beverley and Bridlington, went through most of the villages in between, even though some of them were quite a distance from the main road. For instance, in Hutton the buses went along Balk Lane, Front Street, Low Green and Back Street, to the main road, and vice-versa. If a bus driver saw a prospective passenger hurrying, he would back down the road to meet him. The East Yorkshire Bus Company timed some of their buses so that they would run just in front of their rivals with the inevitable result. A few years later the East Yorkshire Bus Company applied to the Traffic Commissioners for permission to run a quarter-hourly summer service between Hull and Scarborough, which was refused.

Just after the First World War Wetherall's ropery closed down. How long the business had existed is obscure, but it was flourishing a century and a half ago, and may have been making halters and ropes long before that. 'Shoo makker maed bearts' were no longer made by the village cobbler. He spent most of his time repairing footwear. Here again the large stores in the towns could sell boots and shoes at a price far below that of the village cobbler. It must be admitted that the shoes from the town suited the fashion-conscious, while those made in the village were not things of beauty, but just made to last.

The 1926 Miners' Strike had little effect on the rural community. There was no electricity in this part of East Yorkshire. It didn't arrive in this parish until 1931. Oil lamps were used for lighting, apart from the very few who could generate their own power. As long as there was a reasonable supply of wood to keep a fire burning for warmth and to heat an oven, that was sufficient. There were no water mains, nor sewers, neither was there a waste disposal service.

At this time there were a few tractors on the farms. The first appeared during the 1914-18 war and were brought from America by the Government. When the war was over there were still as many horses on farms, and even a farm of seven or eight hundred acres often possessed only one tractor which was used mostly for threshing. Most people of that time were not mechanically minded, whether they belonged to the town or country, and old customs die hard; for example, when Bridlington's horse buses were scrapped and replaced by a motorised fleet, one rebellious driver filled the radiator with oats. The driver of a tractor sometimes forgot to stamp on the clutch, shouted 'whoa' instead, and went through a hedge into the next field. At this time petrol was 11 ½d a gallon, and tractor vapourising oil (paraffin) was 5 ½ a gallon for two hundred gallons. Diesel oil was practically unknown. There was only a very small amount of fuel and lubricating oil used by the few tractors and even less lubricating oil by the grass reapers and binders.

The wagons and carts were greased with grease from the nearest ketyard. The old portable steam engines were still in use on the farms, and I can remember one replacing a tractor for threshing. The total spent on oil of any kind on even a large farm was quite small, on others practically nil.

So, half a century and more ago the villager, or countryman, was left more or less to his own devices, and even though there were motor cars in the country as well as in the towns, he could to a certain extent stand on one side as the world went by.

In 1920 the Parish Council asked the Driffield Rural District Council to build houses suitable for agricultural workers, and in 1925 a few were built along Hutton Road. Prior to that the District Council had asked the Parish Council if the barn at Hutton on the farm which the Parish Council had recently acquired could be converted to houses. Apparently the Driffield Rural were not going to throw the ratepayers' money about.

In 1929 agricultural land was de-rated, which was supposed to help the industry, but didn't in fact make any difference. A committee has been considering reimposing these rates, but has decided against it as this would increase the cost of food.

In 1920 wheat was 94s. per quarter, which was quite a good price. By 1925 it was 44s. and barley was 36s. 1929 was quite a good year with a fine summer and a reasonable harvest with wheat and barley at 36s. per quarter.

Fat bullocks were £15, £24 and £26. Many were sold at 30s. per hundredweight live weight; some even less. Cows in milk were £15 to £20.

Much has been written about this period as being the 'roaring twenties', or as being one of the worst periods in British history. Others refer to it as the 'good old days', but the truth must lie somewhere in between. Some call it the 'good old days' because it was often the halcyon days of their youth, and they look back on it through rose-tinted spectacles and forget the hardships.

At this time unemployment was growing but most of the people were reasonably well-dressed, though it must be admitted that those with families found it not so easy. In those days there were no child allowances. Still, conditions were far better than those of the early part of the century when two boys left Cranswick school early to collect soup from South Hall for the family. The Old Age Pensions had made life a little better for the elderly and where, in the century before, Mary Petch had doctored her neighbours to the best of her ability, the Health Service had taken over.

Most of the people of this parish were on the panel of Dr Keith or Dr Burgess. Dr Keith retired in 1926 and was followed by Dr Milner. Dr Keith was a respected Doctor who lived at Driffield, and his henchman, or 'chuckerout' (or 'in'), was a chap called Con Pickering, who marshalled the patients in the surgery waiting room. He was a little man who walked on his heels and greeted everyone with a baleful glare. Once he received a verbal message asking the doctor to visit a woman with a stomach complaint. Con said 'Keep walking her aboot an ahl send Keith when he cums'. One of the ways of alleviating 'gripes', or indigestion, in horses was to keep them walking.

At that time the nearest hospital, in fact the only one, was the small Cottage Hospital in Bridlington Road, Driffield. It was simply a converted house and when the Alfred Bean Hospital was built in 1931, it reverted to a private house again. The little Cottage Hospital could only accommodate a few patients and many were sent to Hull Infirmary, the building which was only recently demolished. Now there are whispers in the wind that the wartime-built Base Hospital and the Alfred Bean may be closed down and all the people requiring treatment sent to Hull or Scarborough. Of course, there is the hospital at Bessingby, Bridlington, which has been going to be built for the last thirty years and now seems as far off as ever.

The coming of radio in the early 'twenties had more impact on the people of the countryside than on the town-dweller. When the newspapers had been the sole disseminators of information, isolated parts of the country often did not know what was going on elsewhere until long after the event. With the advent of radio, or 'wireless' as it was called, news could be flashed instantly to the remotest parts of the United Kingdom. These old radio sets were very primitive. Some of them needed a pole as large as a small tree to carry an outside aerial. Their range too was limited.

The population of the parish remained more or less static. The 1921 figures were 961 as against 967 in 1911.

1921, Various Excise Licences:

Carriage drawn by four horses	£2. 2s. 0d
Carriage drawn by one horse	£1. 1s. 0
Motor cars not exceeding 6h.p.	£6. 0s. 0d

At this time the motor car was appearing on the country roads in increasing numbers, but there were still a certain amount of horsedrawn vehicles.

1921, Postage stamps used by the general public for letters and postcards cost ½ d, 1d, 1 ½d, and 2d.

1921, Health Insurance Benefits: Sick pay 15s. per week for twenty-six weeks for a man, and 12s. per week for a woman. Disablement benefits were 7s. 6d. per week commencing twenty-six weeks from the beginning of the illness and continuing as long as the disablement lasted, or until the age of 70. Practically all the workers of either sex between the ages of 16 and 70 whose wages did not amount to more than £250 a year came under the National Insurance Act. Insurance contributions for a man were 5d. per week and his employer paid another 5d. Anyone going sick and drawing benefit was said to be on 'Lloyd George'. A worker who became his own master could lose his contributions unless he took out a self-employed card. In most villages the Oddfellows and the Foresters Clubs were dispensing sickness benefit long before the National Insurance Act, but only on a small scale, as their funds were limited.

1921, Income Tax:

A single person earning £150 a year was exempt.

A single person earning £155 a year paid 13s. 6d.

A married man without children earning £286 a year paid £4. 1s. 0d.

A married man with three children earning £380 a year paid £4. 1s. 0d.

Super tax was paid on incomes over £2,000 a year.

By the end of 1921 the post-war boom had collapsed and the farm workers were earning 9d. an hour and the tradesmen not much more. One shilling an hour was a good wage. Threshing wages for a nine-hour day were 8s. and 1s. extra for the corn carriers, so Income Tax didn't bother most of the people of this parish or district unduly whether employed on the land or elsewhere. Like the farmer we heard about previously, most of them were more concerned with 'outgo'.

CHAPTER TWENTY

THE HINDING AND HIRING SYSTEM

Many of the agricultural historians quote Henry Best of Elmswell, near Driffield, in the seventeenth century as hiring men at Malton for 2s.6d. to 3s. per week for one year. They then became part of the household for the following year, but ate with the farmer, who presided at the head of the table. There is no mention of the 'hinding' system, which was so common throughout East Yorkshire. Most of this would start with the Enclosures of the eighteenth, and in the case of the Wolds, the nineteenth century.

'Hind' is Anglo-Saxon and one dictionary says it means a rustic, ploughman, bondager or hand. This was not true of the hind or foreman of the nineteenth or early twentieth century in East Yorkshire: he was more or less a manager and next to the farmer had charge of the farm and the men, with the exception of the beastman and shepherd, who were always directly responsible to the master, and woe betide the foreman who meddled in their affairs. The foreman was always called 'boss' and the master 'gaffer'. If a stranger had come to the farm and asked any of the men for the boss, he would have been sent to the foreman, when in all probability he would have been seeking the master. It was sometimes said that it was a poor farm which could not support two idle men; the farmer and his foreman. This was not really true as most farmers preferred the idle men to be themselves.

On the small farms the hired men were usually boarded by the master himself as in Henry Best's day. The farms were bigger in the Wolds, the farmers better off, and they didn't want to be bothered with men living in, and so the gentleman farmer was born. He would engage a foreman who would board the men at so much per head per week. A foreman who had taken on the 'mearting' of men was said to be going 'hinding'.

This parish stretches on to the foothills of the Wolds, but the farms were smaller, as they still are, with not so many foremen acting as hinds. Thus, to get an accurate picture we must digress a little and refer to the big farms on the chalk hills of the Wolds.

Usually the farmer who fed and boarded the men himself kept a better 'meart hoose' than did the hind, who in the period between the two world wars received only 7s. to 9s. per week per head, for feeding the men and lads. Most of them were aged from 15 or 16 years up to 23 or 24 and were all the same price whatever their eating capacities. The employer supplied the beds and bedding as well as the crockery, milk and potatoes. On many large farms the hind house was quite a distance from the master's house as he did not want to be kept awake by some of the lads returning home late at night full of ale and song. On some of the smaller holdings where there was a large rambling house, one end was often converted into a hind house.

This had to be large enough to accommodate all the hired men, often twelve or more in number all the year through. (this only applied to the large farms), and also the one or two extras in the summer months and the foreman, his wife, and domestic help who worked unlimited hours for a few shillings a week and keep. In harvest time there were often six or seven Irish harvesters. These had beds made up in the granary, but got all their food in the hind's house.

The foreman's wife was not responsible for washing the clothes of her boarders. They had to take it home or, if too far away, find someone to do it. I remember a story of a lad whose home was eight miles from the place where he was hired, who used to walk part of the distance homewards; another member of the family set off to meet him. They were supposed to meet more or less half way. The lad changed his 'shet' behind the nearest hedge; it would be the only thing he would have to change; donned his clean apparel and walked back towards his place of work.

Often the hinds were on the move when Martinmas Day came round (23 November) and it was said of some of them that they were going round the Wolds for the second time, while others remained with one employer for the greater part of their working lives. They were paid weekly, but Martinmas was the time for moving unless they had a row with their employer, when they had to get out as soon as possible. It usually got round whether a foreman kept a 'meart hoose'. Some of them were quite good, others not so good, and a minority pretty rotten. With being paid so little, the hinds' wives must have accomplished miracles to keep the men reasonably well fed and have a bit of profit left. Even with a domestic help there was a lot of hard work involved and trips to the nearest town were few and far between. The wives' only means of locomotion, if they hadn't a bicycle, was borrowing the farm's 'horse float', provided they had their husband or someone else to drive them. The 'float hoss' was often a half-bred animal which could also be used in the field. It was sometimes a frisky, high-mettled creature which was liable to go through the nearest hedge if it met anything it didn't like and was not suitable for a woman driver.

Prior to the First World War, the men in the hind house were given quite a lot of milk, which is a complete food in itself. Tea then became popular and tough meat and hard pies became the principal parts of a meal. Meat pies made of 'long' pastry were a good standby and others filled with figs, prunes, dates, or rhubarb if there was any on the farm. Very little of this was grown on the Wolds.

During the 1920s when sugar beet growing was being encouraged by the Government, a gang of miners was sent to a farm on the High Wolds to hoe the beet. This was a last resort when crop and rubbish were growing fast, as their work left much to be desired. They would be sent by the Employment Exchange and would lose their 'dole' if they refused. If such a thing were proposed today, there would be a national strike, however high the unemployment. The miners were quartered in the hind house and received the same food as the hired men. This did not seem much to their liking as they began to ask where were all the eggs and bacon they had expected.

Rider Haggard once visited Eastburn, near Driffield, and was given some meat pie, which he pronounced substantial and good. Whether this was one specially baked, or just the same as the chaps in the foreman's house got their teeth into, we don't know. There were some tall tales told of these pies; how some of them had been tied behind a wagon for ten miles and were still intact at the end. As Rider Haggard said, they were substantial and good, provided they were made right. The same could be said of all the others made of figs, prunes, dates, etc., that is, if you could stand the sight and taste of them day after day for a year on end. Of course, there were what were called 'pot on days', when there was broth and dumplings. These usually occurred about twice a week, always on the same days.

To be fair to the hinds they, or their wives, they had to cut costs to the bone. Often some of them had taken on the job at too low a price and if they had started off with good intentions and 'short pastry' they soon found they were losing money. In any case the hired lads could have eaten the 'small pastries': them things et you can crush i yer and', as one of them put it, by the barrow load. Due to being in the open air so much and subject to those socalled 'lazy' winds on the Wolds which don't bother to go round you but go straight through, most of them with their knees under the hind house table got so hungry they could almost have eaten a bale of straw. At that time in the rural areas bread, like the pastry, was home baked and flour was 4s.9d. for four stone. Breakfast cereals were unheard of.

The beef bacon never appeared on a hind house table was bought in large quantities and was nearly always the cheapest cuts. There were no fridges or freezers in those days, at least not in the country districts, and where there were a lot of mouths to feed, it meant buying sufficient to last until the butcher's next visit. The meat got a bit blue, often nearly black, in the warm days of summer and sometimes smelled a bit high, but it was very seldom any was wasted.

Keeping the hinds stocked up with cheap beef was good business and some butchers did quite well out of it, as a continuous supply was needed throughout the year. Apart from this, it provided them with an outlet for low grade joints which more fastidious customers would not buy. One butcher who did a big trade with the hinds invited them all to his premises every Christmas, where he gave them a first-rate meal. One man I knew well remembers when he was a young lad hired at Kelleythorpe, near Driffield. The time would be near the end of the last century; maybe just before Rider Haggard sampled the meat pie at the next farm, Eastburn. This is what he said:

> D'ord foreman used ti fetch'd meart fra Thriffield in a cloes basket. Ah cudn't eart it, it was nowt but auld coo ure. Ah used ti pur it i me pocket for'd cats. D'ord Cats was allus waitin for ma when ah gor outside. Me pocket gor all black and breet.
> (coo ure = cow udder)

He lived to be over ninety. Nobody seemed to suffer any ill effects from this rough diet, and ulcers were practically unknown. Today in a more affluent society, we are always being warned of the danger to health of the present-day diet.

All the hired lads (they were all called lads, though I remember one over 60), most of them horsemen, went into their meals in their proper order. 'Wag' went first, and the others trailed behind in order of superiority with the young lads bringing up the rear. There was no talking allowed and often the whole process only took ten minutes. Indeed, there was a popular joke that when one of the young lads at Cowlam, then at 1500 acres the biggest farm on the Yorkshire Wolds, 'tummeled' (fell), by the time he had gathered himself up the others were coming out. The foreman presided over the meal and carved all the meat, if it could be called carving, as one man, recalling the days of his youth on a large farm, said it was just hacked off in chunks. At the evening meal 'wag' was in charge of the carving.

On most of the big farms the hired men were not supposed to be in the house except for eating and sleeping. The rest of the time they had to be in what was called the 'slum'. This was a horse box or similar building which had a fireplace installed. The usual furniture was what was called a 'long settle', which was just a seat with a high back. On this high back, cut with a knife, were recorded the names of past 'wags', 'thods' and others who had spent their nights there. This was a kind of ritual.

Needless to say, there was always a roaring fire as the coals were 'ad lib'. If they were ever locked up the door was soon broken down.

On many of the Wold farms there was no supply of fresh water, and it was often a case of using soft water or rainwater from a cistern. As this was supplied from the roofs of the house and buildings, the water used to stink in a warm, dry summer and even when boiled for making tea, it had a decided 'pong'. This was not surprising as dead birds and their excreta were washed off the roofs into the cistern. In a wet season when there was a good supply of water flowing into the tank, it was a great deal fresher. It seems a miracle there was no outbreak of typhoid, though the process of boiling to make tea would sterilise the water to a certain extent. Even then the smell was still there.

In a dry summer water-carting was a costly and time consuming business, and when the dewponds began to get low one man on a farm often did nothing else but 'lead' water for the stock from the nearest village or anywhere else. It didn't matter about the quality and often it was more like thick chalky mud. Those villages known as the 'Dearl Toons', Weaverthorpe, Luttons, etc., once had the Gypsey Race as their main supply of water. This spring-fed stream gushing out of the hillside in Warram Percy Dale was later tapped by the local authority, and where it runs through the villages it is now very much polluted.

All hiring agreements terminated on 23 November, Martinmas Day, excluding the hiring for harvest agreements, which were one month. 11 November is the real Martinmas Day, and in some counties this was the day when the statute hirings were held so the worker on the farm must have left his employment in the early part of the month. But in East Yorkshire, 23 November was the day he left the place where he had worked for twelve months, or if he was satisfied, stayed on for another. Often when it got to harvest time, some of the younger ones began counting the days and weeks to Martinmas. Others, if they were fed up with the place, a good deal earlier.

There was one hirings day about ten days before 23 November, when a day off was allowed to attend it. Often there was not a great deal of hiring done. Most, whether employed or employer, preferred to wait until the next one in Martinmas week, unless there was someone willing to offer a higher wage than the average for that area. Of course, there was always a way out for anyone who had undertaken to work for a year on a certain farm. If he gave his 'fest' back before he started work the deal was off. Nothing was ever put in writing and if it had been suggested that it should be anything but verbal, there would have been hardly any hiring done. The 'fest', at one time only a shilling or two, in this century got to be ten shillings or sometimes even a pound, and always clinched the deal.

'Fest' is from the Danish 'Faestepenge', or Godespenny, and is said to be used only in connection with servants hired under the Martinmas system. Hiring in most cases was the foreman's task and if he wanted any hired man to stop again, he asked him well before Martinmas Day. Otherwise he said nothing and those he wanted rid of had to seek pastures new on 23 November. Sometimes it fell on a Monday and at one time a few farmers wouldn't pay their men off on a Saturday but insisted on keeping them until Monday afternoon. Legally they were entitled to do this, but it was rather a miserly attitude and didn't improve relations between master and man.

There were grievances on both sides. There was a case in this parish well into this century where a farmer asked his man to fetch a load of rubble from a building site. He came back empty because there was no one to help him load his vehicle. Nothing was said at the time and the chap fully expected he would be stopping on again when Martinmas came round. He got a big surprise on being told he wouldn't be needed any more and the refusal to load the rubble was brought up.

There were hirings at Driffield, Beverley, Hunmanby and Beeford at the beginning of this century. At Driffield they lingered on into the 1930s, though the hiring as it used to be had practically gone. The Wages Board was set up in 1924, though all hiring contracts were settled by mutual agreement. Martinmas was at one time just a week, and when it got to be a few more days after the First World War, it was thought to be the end of all things. It was also a time for buying clothes, boots and settling bills. Most tradesmen could give a certain amount of credit for goods bought during the year. It was possible to have what was called a 'sub' where the employer let the employed have an advance on his yearly wage. When he was said to be 'subbed up', he had drawn all the money he had earned.

If a hired lad was sick of his place, one old dodge was to draw as much money as possible and decamp silently during the night. Most of the farmers were hard-bitten types and that dodge seldom worked. Some lads would go to a fresh place of work and not liking it much would go for good after a day or two. It was essential not to be encumbered with too much baggage. As one farmer said, 'Ya cum wi yer pillarcases, but ya dearn't stop lang'. The usual receptacle for clothes was a stout wooden box about three or four feet long by two wide. That was for those who intended staying their full year and was the only place for clothes when their owner wasn't wearing them. There were no luxuries such as wardrobes; even pegs were very few. These old boxes, some of them a good deal battered, did not always contain clothes. One middle-aged man who wasn't quite 'jannock' had his full of horse collars and harness.

Under the 1867 Master and Servant Act cases came before the Courts where the employer claimed damages for broken yearly hiring contracts. In one case heard at Driffield Magistrates Court in 1874 the defendant left because of the hard bed. His employer said the bed had been changed and wished to have the man back. The Court decided he should pay £1 compensation and 20s.6d. to be deducted from his wages, so I suppose justice was not only done but seen to be done, to use a phrase beloved of the legal profession. Fifty years later some of those beds were just as hard and seemed to be just a mass of lumps. It was a case of getting draped between the lumps then you might get a reasonable night's sleep. The Indian fakirs and their beds of nails had nothing on those rock-like contraptions, though very few hired lads suffered from insomnia.

An M. Baron was also charged at the Driffield Court with absconding from the service of his master, H. Moor of Watton Carr. He had to pay 18s. costs and his master agreed to take him back. 18s. was a big sum out of a wage of possibly £20.

Those relics of the feudal days lingered on well into the twentieth century, and even in 1940 there was a case of a young man of 24 who, while working on a farm near an aerodrome, had a narrow escape from German bombs and his doctor said he should leave the farm as his nerves were being affected. After he had left the farm manager sent him a letter threatening to sue for breach of contract as he had been engaged from Martinmas to Martinmas, though he was paid weekly. Of course, no Court would have looked twice at such a man. It was just a 'try on', and was the last dying kick of the yearly hirings.

From 1918 onwards, if a hired man wished to leave his employer, he would be paid the money he had earned up to date without much quibbling. To have a reluctant worker about the place could cause many problems as most farmers realised.

I remember my father saying that one farmer who lived at Neswick. near Bainton, in the 1880s, used to get the hired lads out of bed at three o'clock in the morning during summer to mow thistles in the grass fields. Needless to say, there was very little work done and they spent most of their time jumping over improvised hurdles made of sticks. The boss, or foreman, who in practically all cases made the decisions about labour, wasn't responsible for it. It may have been that he was a single foreman living in the master's house and had to go along with the others. This may have been an isolated case as even at that period of the nineteenth century in most instances the farmer would have been told in no uncertain terms what he could do. This kind of serfdom was said by some who could remember those days to be responsible for the Wold Rangers and other tramps who wandered about the Wolds. Most of them had been hired and decided that the roving life was much better than being tied for a year and working all the hours their employers decreed. They had their freedom. All they needed was a bit of food and their clothes would last for years. There were always odd jobs to be done on a farm, such as going into the sheep fold for a while in winter. If they got sick of this after earning a little money, moving on presented no problems. As for sleeping quarters, they knew all the best places in the farm buildings and where there was plenty of straw for a bed. The occupier of a farm, or his foreman, always knew if there was a tramp on the premises. If he was a smoker he was relieved of his matches in case he set himself and the whole farmstead on fire.

Before the First World War, the young lad who had just left school at fourteen 'fost year off' was usually the butt for everyone else, including the foreman. What with eating the tough meat and hard pies in a few minutes, plus dodging the foreman's boot he often had a pretty miserable time. When the foreman had finished his meal he got up from the table: the others had to do likewise. If the unfortunate 'learst lad', as he was often called, hadn't finished his meal he had to leave it.

> On August 8th, 1860, at Driffield Magistrates Court, John Noble, farm foreman for Mr Moore, Burn Butts, Cranswick, was charged with assaulting Henry Train, a lad in his employ. There were severe stripes on his back. A summons was granted.

That report came from the Driffield Times. Even fifty years later the position was not so much different, and I can remember a man telling how as a young lad the foreman, when showing him how to use a scruffler, spent most of an afternoon kicking his behind. He said 'bunched' it; that word is still used in East Yorkshire you don't kick anything, you 'bunch' it, and it is only done to or by humans. It never applies to animals and if you are the receiving end of a kick from an animal it is just a kick. This policy of kicking the young lad's rear end was rather short-sighted as when he got to be a man he often gave the foreman a good hiding. This sometimes happened at the hirings where they settled grudges after getting well primed with beer. One foreman, a stoutish chap, was said to knock a lad down then roll over him. Another one kicked the 'learst lad's' behind every morning before breakfast. That was supposed to set him on the right lines for the day.

Many school leavers put in a year or two on the smaller lowland farms before moving on to the higher and drier Wolds. There was a lot more prestige in being a 'wag' at Cowlam or some other large farm than one in Hutton Cranswick parish, which would often be referred to as a 'lartle lad spot'.

Hutton Mill, c. 1905.

Hunt and followers at Hutton Mill, c. 1905Church Road, c. 1912.

Church Road c. 1912.

Post Office, Church Road, Hutton, c. 1950.

Jubilee House (on left) owned by Ken Richardson, c. 1950.

Hutton pump, c. 1905.

Mill Street, Hutton, c. 1906.

The Old Vicarage, top of Howl Lane.

St Peter's Church, Hutton.

CHAPTER TWENTY-ONE

THE HORSE ON THE FARM

The wagoner had his pick of the horses on the farm. The younger lads got the older and not so good animals. The reshuffle, if one was needed, took place during Martinmas week. It wasn't very good policy to take a good horse from one lad and give him one not so good when he had already taken charge of it. It was sometimes done in mid-year if anyone had left and before a new arrival took over. This quite often caused a bit of ill-feeling later. A good set of horses on a farm were an added attraction. It usually got round, like the 'meart hoose', whether such and such a farm possessed a good set of horses, and often gave a farmer that extra bit of bargaining power at hiring time.

Up to the First World War. the Shires, or Shiretype horses were the main breed on the Wolds or the lowlands. There were also some Clydesdales. Then came a few Suffolk Punches or Suffolk crosses with a few Percherons from France. These were all lighter with very little hair on the legs and were said to need less feed to keep them in first-class condition. These caught on to a certain extent, but mechanisation was just around the corner. Many of the Wold farms had 18 to 20 horses. Wag had six, and a lad. He was known as 'wag lad'. Then 'thoddy' (third lad) also had six and a lad; 'thoddy lad'. 'Fourt' (fourth lad) had four to himself, as had 'fiver' (fifth lad). On the largest farms there was also a sixth lad, 'sixer'. Cowlam had approximately thirty horses. Wag had eight and two lads; 'thoddy' had the usual six and a lad; then came 'fourt', 'fiver', 'sixer' and 'seventher' (seventh lad), who all had four each. Apart from these there was always the odd one or two used by the shepherd or beastman for pulling the turnip cutter in the sheepfold in winter or leading roots. Incidentally, Cowlam was broken up in the late 1920s.

Wag, or thod, fed all the horses in their care and brushed and cleaned their own particular pair. Grooming, as it is called nowadays, was brushing. If wag lad had been told 'Groom them osses', he would have wondered what it meant. If it had been 'Brush them osses ower', he would have known instantly. The lad did most of the mucking out, carried the straw in and 'brushed' the remaining four. The only time he was allowed to feed them was the weekend when the wag had gone home. Horse feeding was quite a skilled job. It was often said that anybody could feed them when they were most of the time in the stable, which was quite true. A novice would often fall into the trap of stuffing them with corn and they certainly would look well. It was a different matter when

March came round and they were hard at work day after day, then they would soon get what was called 'stalled'; that meant they ate a good deal less than they should and 'swealed away ti nowt'. They often remained on the thin side until May when Doctor Green (i.e. grass), that curer of so many live stock ailments, took over. An experienced feeder always kept his horses on the hungry side until February, then when they were put into hard work they suffered no ill effects.

It was a point of honour to keep the horses in as good condition as possible, and to give them plenty of time to eat a good meal. It was sometimes said when a 'wag' went by on the road with a wagon and four horses in firstclass condition, 'He varry near stops up wiv em all neet'. There was another side to this and drugs were sometimes administered to them to 'sharpen up' the appetite. This was a dangerous practice and quite illegal, as this abridged extract from the Driffield Times of 24 February 1912 shows:

> Horse poisoning case at Driffield:
>
> Mr Foley, Field House, Driffield, summoned G. Gardham for administering drugs to horses. The horses had begun to look remarkably well from about August until November when the man left. About a week after that the horses went off their feed and December 31st one was found dead. The same day another one died. On January 4th, the other two died. A mixture of arsenic, antimony and aniseed was found among chaff. The vet had found some of this in the animals' stomachs. The case was proved and the defendant was fined £5 under the new Act framed to deal with such cases. The Magistrate said it seemed to be a common practice in some districts.

£5 would be about a fourth of G. Gardham's yearly wage. His old employer would also suffer severe financial loss, apart from the cruelty to the animals. Even after the First World War there was a bit of this done though the case above may have been an extreme one. After Martinmas some horses lost condition and nothing would improve it. That could be an indication, more so if the previous horseman had left at Martinmas, that they had been given some drugs the previous year.

All the horse feeding was completely unpaid until just before the Second World War started. The hired horse lads, like the weekly men, worked from six to six with the exception of Saturday, when they finished at five o'clock. On top of that the horse lads often got upat four in the morning to feed and clean their charges ready for when boss shouted 'Ger em oot wag'. After tea it could often take them until eight o'clock; after that their time was their own. Just before the Second World War it was ruled that all work outside ordinary working hours, such as horse feeding, should be paid.

'Gooin oot wid wagin' meant brushing and polishing, 'Scotch bobbing' and rig plaiting all the horses. On the large farms there were special 'Scotch topped' collars, wagon breech bands, quarter straps and backband traces, which were carefully oiled or blacked before being put away until needed again. These were never used on ordinary land work. Four Shires in a wagon all decked up in their Sunday best with all the head and other brasses shining made an impressive sight going through a town. We see a similar spectacle at some of the large agricultural shows when some of the Brewery Companies put on a display. This is purely for advertisement. The driver sits on the top with a handful of reins in his hands, whereas the true East Yorkshireman always sat on the near or lefthand side of the rear pair, the saddle horse, and drove the front pair, the 'fost hosses', with reins. The one in the 'far wheel' was tied to the saddle horse so he couldn't get far out of line. This was a far more efficient method than being hampered with a handful of reins. It was surprising how well four went together as they were nearly always in the same position and knew what was expected of them. A good driver could cut right into a hedge bottom when opening out a field of corn with a binder. There were always some horses who were a bit troublesome. Often a perfectly matched four would be spoilt by one which may have been inclined to kick, so out it had to go.

'Gooin oot wid wagin' often meant 'liverin', that is, taking corn to the nearest railway station or town. Often four wagons were loaded in the stackyard during threshing. The next day wag, thod, fourth and fiver, 'livvered' the wagon loads, with their sixteen horses looking their very best, to the nearest corn factor's depot. After harvest there was often a week of what was called 'threshin and livvering'. The corn was thrashed in the stackyard and loaded on the wagons at the same time. Wag and thod often did nothing else but take them to unload and bring back the empty ones. At one time a tremendous amount of corn was put on rail at all the stations between Driffield and Malton. Fimber, now derelict, had a large privately-owned corn warehouse in the station yard.

A few of the larger Wold farms had what was called an 'off spot' or 'wauld spot' situated in some isolated fields. This would be on top of a hill. Here there would be a fold yard for bullocks, and a granary or barn for holding corn or cattle feed, and in some cases a house as well. Often a week's thrashing of corn was stacked there from nearby fields and thrashed just after harvest. The bullocks were then put in the yard and lived on straw and roots until the spring. This method saved a great deal of labour both at harvest and during the winter months. The muck in the yards was just where it was needed and didn't need to be dragged up the hill from the farmstead lower down.

Sir Mark Sykes of Sledmere realised the potential of the horsemen from East Yorkshire when he formed the Wagoners' Reserve before the First World War. They were ready-made artillery and supply wagon drivers who were enlisted and paid a kind of retaining fee. Many of them didn't realise what they were letting themselves in for. There were thirteen local Wagoners' Reservists, most of them from Cranswick, enrolled before the First World War. The ordinary driver got a £1 retainer. A man who got a few more to enrol received £2, and when called up was given the rank of corporal. One of these who got a few to sign up kept telling them, 'Cum on, it's money for nowt', and so it seemed after they had had a few pints of beer.

When they were called up, which to most of them was quite unexpected, they boarded the five o'clock train to Driffield. There they had to wait for a train to Bradford. One of them who had been sozzled for about a week said, 'Ah's hungry', and pulled a handful of cold beans and bacon out of his pocket, but he couldn't get it steered into his mouth. Finally, he got it in the region of one ear and slid it down into his mouth. With the other he got on the train to Bradford. It is said that he didn't remember much until he found himself kitted out and being bawled at by a Sergeant Major on a parade ground in France. Meanwhile, the man who got them enrolled, now a fully-fledged Corporal, went with them to Driffield to see them off, as he was the only one who hadn't received call-up papers. As the train pulled out of the station for Bradford he shouted, 'Ahl searn be after ya lads'. He went sooner than he expected as his call-up papers were waiting for him when he got home.

Those Wagoners were the despair of the drill Sergeant, though they admitted that if any drivers were required they could drive anything anywhere, and that was what they signed on for. They were engaged on a yearly basis and like the yearly hirings their contracts were renewed annually. Just a few of those thirteen didn't sign on again and came back to work on the farms.

When conscription was introduced later, they had to stay in the army until the war ended. There is a memorial to the Wagoners at Sledmere showing their activities in the field before 1914 and after.

A few of them ended up as infantrymen and some of the scenes on the Memorial showing Germans being skewered by British bayonets were not very popular with the Nazis just before World War Two. A party of them delivered a strong protest to the Foreign Office, which I suppose made the usual soothing noises. Even in those days of appeasement and weak-kneed Government they must have stood firm as the Memorial remained the same. The many German prisoners in that area, 1944 and onwards, would have had to look at it when they went to work on the Wold farms. It seems a kind of poetic justice.

As the tractors came in the horses went out, and with them the long hours involved. The image of the farm worker also improved and he became more like a mechanic. Today, the rare occasions when horses are at work in the fields arouse a great deal of nostalgia.

In spring time, one of the busiest seasons of the year, horses often suffered from what was called 'maned'. That meant sore shoulders and they were sometimes worked when they should not have been. After fifteen or twenty years' faithful service, most of them became what were known as 'swimmers', that meant they were sent on the hoof to the Continent where they were slaughtered for human consumption.

In hot weather the horses were plagued by flies, especially so in the carrs of the lowlands where they were pestered by the 'clegs' (horse flies) in summer. These were never seen on the Wolds. These flies always appeared near streams and were hardly ever seen on the higher ground above Cranswick station. I don't think anyone in farming wants the horses back, apart from the economic reasons.

I often wonder what the authorities would consider necessary safety precautions for working with horses, if you could transpose all the present-day regulations back in time to those years when the horse was supreme. There are no figures to prove it, but I should think there were more accidents than in the present mechanised age. Then they got a great deal less publicity. A kick in the right, or the wrong, place could mean the end for the individual who received it. This was not always due to bad temper on the part of the animal, though if its ears went back it was advisable to keep away from the rear end. It was seldom it used its forefeet.

Accidents could be caused by a horse being startled. Often it was sheer exuberance, more so when the animal was in good condition and not doing much work. Young horses were sometimes as 'kittle as moosetraps', an expression used when they were inclined to 'gallop away' or bolt if a bird flew out of a hedge. In such circumstances anyone loading a wagon could be thrown off behind causing serious injuries.

Practically all self binders were 'left-hand cut'. That meant the driver of the three or four horses was riding the one nearest the knife, which could be dangerous and led to some fatal accidents. It was often suggested that all binders should be made to cut the other way round. The driver, if his horses got out of control,, could always jump off and be clear of the knife. In these circumstances there might even have been some primitive method of baling out, or we could have had statutory measures enforcing the cutting down of the horses feed so that they were not so fresh. Complete with an army of inspectors to see that no one stepped out of line.

1925: here are a few figures showing the cost of labour involved in sowing 140 acres of winter wheat on a 900 acre Wold farm by ploughing and pressing. In a wet autumn this was,, and still is, the best method of sowing; as all the ploughing, drilling and harrowing was completed in one operation. There was no land left partly worked down to get wet and unsowable. Today most of the old press drills have gone for scrap.

Implements used:
3	double furrow ploughs
1	single plough
1	three-sheaf press
1	four-sheaf press
2	sets of harrows.

Horses used:
11	ploughing
2	in three-sheaf press
3	in four-sheaf press
4	in two sets of harrows

Total: 20

Men engaged:
4	ploughing
2	pressing
2	harrowing

Total: 8

Hired men's wages:
Wag	£46 yearly
Thod	£36
Fourt	£32
Fiver	£30
Wag lad	£28
Thoddy lad	£25
Tommy Owt	£46
Total:	£243

(the foreman made up the eight)

The foreman would be on a weekly wage of 38s. a week. On some farms it may have been more, on others less. At that time a 9 ½ hour day was being worked in the field. Wag's wages would work out about 3s.6d. per day plus the 1s. a day the farmer paid the foreman for his keep. All those feeding horses would put in a total of 12 ½ hours daily, excluding Saturday and Sunday. Their weekly hours would be in the region of 65. This does not include work done during the dinner hour such as getting straw in, feeding, etc., so if we take the wag's wage as a basis and include all the others with a lower wage, we get eight men and lads working for 3 ½d an hour. The cost to the farmer of one man for one day was 4/6d, 36s for eight men for one day. There was also an insurance stamp, 5d. which was paid by the employer and the same amount by the employee. The twenty horses would be valued at £600 to £700. They all lived on home-grown produce.

Those eight men and twenty horses would sow about six acres a day. Today one man with a tractor could do the same. It could cost £7,000 to £15,000 and runs on imported fuel. The driver would earn far more in a week than his counterpart over fifty years ago earned in one year. Incidentally, those double furrow ploughs or 'double deckers', as they were always called, were only used on that particular farm when ploughing and pressing. They were very seldom used on even light land farms as they took too much of a 'pull'.

The horseman needed good feet. If he hadn't and couldn't 'foller hosses' he had to take some other job such as 'bullocky' (looking after the bullocks) or a 'sheepford navvy' (a 'sheepford navvy' worked in the sheep fold all winter pulling swedes and cutting them up for fattening sheep or hoggs). Spring time often found out those with bad feet.

In the earlier part of this century when turnips were grown as part of a rotation, all the drills had shafts and the shaft horse was led by a drill stick which was fastened to its bit rings. On the lowlands there were never more than two horses in a drill. On the Wolds for many years the drills were four rowed: with one shaft horse and two in front. I was told by some of the farm workers (born about 1870) that at one time the 'learst lad' walked between the 'fost bosses' and led them. This must have been extremely dangerous for the lad as, when the whole outfit turned round at the end, he could have been trodden on or knocked down. In those days lads were expendable, but I was told it was made illegal and ever after the two horses in front were always driven.

Neighbouring farms often vied with one another as to who could drill the straightest rows of turnips. When these were sown in May the rows, whether straight or crooked, showed up until harvest; then they 'met id row and almost looked as if they had been broadcast.

I remember my father telling a tale of how a man from another farm was going to show them how 'drill leading' should be done. He seems to have been a bit of a bighead. Part of the field was already drilled and he was going to show how much straighter his rows could be. He took hold of the drill stick and set off up the field. There was always a drill follower who walked behind and saw there were no seed blockages; so father walked behind the drill. When they got to the brow of the hill in the middle of the field he grabbed one of the wheels and gave it a great pull. There was a great deal of shouting from the man leading the drill, but he couldn't see anything as the horse obscured his view. When they got to the end and turned round, there in full view of the road was a large 'jibble' bend. The man who was trying to show how drilling should be done said 'This auld mear rolls waintly'. All he got in reply was 'She dis sumtarms', and he retired suitably deflated.

Today the tractor driver needs a well-sprung seat to protect his rear end and ear muffs to shut out the rattling and the 'diesel knock'. By law he must have a safety cab to protect him if his machine overturns. Noise is tiring and he will often get more tired, but in a different way from the man who walked behind his horses and plough. The only sounds he heard were the squeak of his plough wheels (depending on whether he oiled them or not), the others talking to their horses and the muted whistle of the soil as it was turned over by the 'slipe' or mouldboard.

Nowhere else in England would you find the pole wagon used as extensively as in East Yorkshire. Elsewhere most of them were equipped with shafts. On the Wolds they were used for almost everything: 'leading' corn at harvest; taking it to the station after it was thrashed, and bedding up the fold yards. Most of them weighed eighteen or nineteen hundredweight empty and the three best were only used for corn and other clean tasks. When wag, thod and fourt had spent a lot of time getting their horses to look their best, it would not do to send them out 'livvering' with decrepit wagons and so they were kept clean and well painted.

A wagon was said to be a good runner when it 'napped' twice after it stopped. That was when the wheels knocked against the pins and bushes holding them on. This gave them a distinctive noise when on the road. There were several local wagon builders. Sissons of Beswick were well known and their vehicles lasted a lifetime. The usual load for a wagon was three or four tons, though it would have carried a great deal more. There was an art in loading it with bags of corn. The usual practice was to start at the front, build up in 'desses' of three and finish at the back end. 'Dess', another old Danish word, means section and it is still used today, though not so much now all hay is baled. When it was stacked loose it was cut down with a hay knife in 'desses'. With this method very little got wet.

A casual observer from another part of England might have thought that shafts were better than poles on a wagon where there were hills, but a couple of good wheel horses with breech bands on could hold a great deal of weight. I remember one wagoner telling a tale of how he went down a steep hill with a load and when he got to the bottom his wheel horses' shoes were hot through holding back the weight. Of course, he was doing what is called 'romancin'' and didn't expect to be taken seriously. Down a steep hill the method of braking was to put on a wagon shoe. This was made of heavy iron and was fastened with a strong chain to the front axle. When not needed it was hung on the underside of the wagon. Coming to a steep hill with a load the wagoner stopped at the top, dropped the shoe in front of the near side hind and drove the wagon on. This dropped the wheel in the shoe; the chain pulled tight; the wheel couldn't turn and this had the desired braking effect. On a long hill the shoe often got hot and wore thin. Then the blacksmith had the job of welding a piece on the underside. Like most things then they were built to last and this didn't happen too frequently. Practically every wagon on the Wolds had one of these contraptions dangling underneath it. On the flat lands of the East Riding you hardly ever saw one.

In Constable's famous picture 'The Hay Wain', the wagon is shown in the middle of a stream. Most countrymen who remember those old vehicles would know instantly what it was there for. With all iron-tyred wagons or carts, it was essential for the rims to be tight on the 'felloes', as the wood section of the wheels were called. In a dry summer the wagons were shoved in a stream or pond to swell the wood and keep the rims from slipping off the wheels. This didn't apply so much to the well-kept wagons of the big farms, but on some of the smaller farms all kinds of devices were used in harvest time to tighten up the wheels. Hammering in a few nails sometimes did the trick. Really the only thing to do was to take them to the blacksmith and get them rehooped and tightened. This could only be done during a slack period. If whoever was in charge of the wagon or cart with a loose tyre didn't keep an eye on it, all the wheel could collapse. If it was the 'learst lad' he might get his rear end 'bunched'. With the coming of the tractor many of the old wagons had a draw bar attached and were rattled along the roads at a speed they were not designed for until they fell apart.

Now those which survive are collector's items. It is amazing how some of these vehicles and machines, ploughs, binders, threshers, etc., most of which were often sworn at by those who wrestled with them and were glad to see their end, have become so popular. Most of the nostalgia seems to come from those who never worked with them, winter and summer, in all kinds of weather. Still, I suppose it is a good thing to keep them if only as a reminder of how far we have progressed in eliminating so much drudgery and as a heritage of our rural past.

CHAPTER TWENTY-TWO

THE DEPRESSION YEARS OF THE 1930S

1930 and 1931 were wet and difficult years for farming. It seemed as if the elements had turned against it and the country in general. We now have what is called roaring inflation. Then we were always in the grip of deflation and the politicians and economists had not the slightest idea of how to deal with it. They were in as big a muddle then as they are today. If all the countryside in England had reverted to waste land, and a fair amount did, it would not have made the slightest difference to the economy of this country. The local labour problems eased a bit, but agriculture remained in the doldrums until 1940. The ramblers could have rambled to their hearts' content. The conservationists who today oppose hedges being pulled up could have watched them rough and uncut, spreading all over the fields. They could have seen the thistles, dockings and all sorts of weeds growing in the fields. The Rural District Council prosecuted owners and tenants of land under the Injurious Weeds Act. Now the boot is on the other foot and the local authorities are the chief offenders. Manor Farm, or Gannock, on the Driffield Road, was derelict for one year, though the rubbish was cut down once. Others were let for a few shillings an acre, if a tenant would be found. A fair amount of the Parish Council land was unlet.

The Wheat Act of 1932 made life a little better for the wheat grower. He had to be registered with a merchant and the wheat had to be of millable quality. Every registered grower could obtain what was called a deficiency payment which was the difference between the standard price and the average price. The standard price was 10s. per hundredweight, equal to 45s per quarter; 32 stones. It was very seldom the grower got 45s. per quarter; it was sometimes £2, and more often he got just over 30s. The miller or merchant who issued the certificate didn't quibble too much about the quality of the wheat as long as it was reasonably dry. After all, the growers were his customers and if he upset them they would soon take their custom elsewhere. Apart from that, many farmers ran up a bill for feeding stuffs and sometimes the only way of getting paid was for the merchant to knock it off the wheat cheque.

In the first year of the Wheat Act, some growers asked their buyers if they would take 'hinderends', small corn. They wouldn't, but most farmers got round that by running the corn 'straight down' the threshing machine and by-passing the riddles which took out the small corn. That satisfied most merchants, as long as the sample was reasonably clean. But the Wheat Act said what had to be sold and removed from the farm to qualify for a deficiency payment. This was not always followed to the letter as some merchants gave a grower a certificate when the wheat was on the farm. A buyer would fetch it and if the grower wished to keep any for stock feed it was left on the premises and he paid the market price for it. This wasn't sharp practice. It just meant cutting out unnecessary transport costs. At that time everything was cut to the bone. I can only remember one prosecution in East Yorkshire under the Wheat Act. In that case wheat had been sold several times and deficiency payments received after every transaction. Penalties were severe and included fines and imprisonment.

The Wheat Act meant that more wheat was sown. All other arable crops were left unsubsidised until just before the War when a scheme was worked out for oats and barley. None of these things did agriculture much good. They were just sops to keep the industry quiet. I remember a farmer in this parish threshing some barley. It was a first class malting sample, for which he had been offered 21s. per quarter. He looked gloomily at the corn as it ran into the bag and said: 'A bloody good fire ud pay as good as owt'.

It was often said at that time that a farm or business premises which were well insured would pay better if it got on fire than to be kept struggling on. And that shows how desperate some people were for a bit of ready cash. Very few would ever think of committing arson. Feeding barley was most of the time under £1 per quarter. Oats were sometimes as low as 11s. Hay could be bought for 15s. to £1 a ton. A few years later in 1941 the brewers were buying any kind of barley for malting. Some of it was hardly fit for feeding to pigs. Malting barley seems hard to define. If there is plenty around the brewers' standards rise, but when there is a shortage, they will take any rubbish.

The banks were very wary of lending money, especially to farmers. As one bank manager said, 'We don't lend money on crops or stock. We don't know who they belong to. We like an insurance policy as security which can be easily cashed'. What he said was quite true. Often the livestock on the farm belonged to a dealer. I remember a tale of that time which may or may not be true. A farmer on a fairly large farm on the Wolds wanted a loan from a bank. Its representative arrived to assess his collateral, or lack of it. As on many farms there were two foldyards with a connecting gate; one was full of bullocks, the other empty. The man from the bank was shown the bullocks and made a note of their value. Then he was taken round the outside of the buildings which obscured his view of them. The farmer's men then drove the bullocks through the connecting gate into the empty yard. When the bank's man got to the other end and looked over the wall, he had seen them twice. Thus in the bank's books the farmer was credited with twice the number of stock he really had. It didn't do him much good as he later went bankrupt, as did another one farming a large farm. He ended up working in the sheep fold for a relative. A young man in quite a small way went more or less bankrupt. Like many more he wasn't bankrupt, 'brokken', only badly bent (those words were often used then). When he had got all cleared up he had sixpence left. He said to his wife 'We'll ev a neet oot on this tanner'.

A tremendous amount of goods were dumped here from all corners of the earth. Much of it from the British Empire. A lot of timber was unloaded at Hull docks at give-away prices. The mills nearby imported a lot of cheap grain, soya beans and maize. It was sometimes said that some of it must have been used for ballasting ships, which may have been true. The makers of compound feeds, dairy cake, sheep nuts, pig feed, etc., increased their trade a great deal. And on the other side of the world the Brazilians were stoking their locomotives on coffee beans as they couldn't get rid of them at any price.

At this time Professor Robert Boutflour was stamping around the countryside preaching his doctrine of no roots, just compounds with a little hay, for milk cows. At this time roots were regarded as an essential part of a cow's ration. Dairy cake was six or seven pounds a ton, often less if bought on contract. Straight cakes such as cotton seed were £3 per ton. Boutflour said it was a waste of time growing roots and feeding them to cows as they were mainly water. He gained a considerable following as more farmers went into milk selling and more land was sown down to grass. All this was based on the assumption that there would always be an unlimited supply of cheap imported food. Like many experts in other fields, Boutflour couldn't see far enough ahead. His ideas, like many British merchant ships, were sunk without trace during the Second World War, when all compound feeds and straight cakes were severely rationed.

In a poll of milk producers conducted by Barton, Mayhew & Co. in 1933, 96% voted in favour of a Milk Marketing Scheme. The milk producers of the 'thirties were like drowning men clutching at straws. When it had been each man for himself he often had to wait for his money. The producer contracted to supply the retailer with a certain amount of milk which had to be strictly adhered to. In May and June when there was plenty of grass the producer might have to buy calves or pigs he didn't want to consume surplus milk.

At that time the dairy firms had the milk seller over a barrel and some of them took advantage of this fact. After announcing a profitable year, one of them said that the supplier would have to take less money. About the only thing a dairy retailing milk firm had to bother about was bad debts. Some of them made the roundsman responsible for the money by deducting from his wages what was outstanding, which made him very careful about any long-winded payers. The same thing applied in the coal trade where two men were sent out with a certain number of bags and were expected to bring the equivalent in money back, or else. This though, was not general practice.

The Milk Marketing Board was set up after the favourable producer vote of 1933. It didn't escape the notice of those who were 'rarving milk oot' (milking cows) at five o'clock in the morning for seven days of the week just to survive that as soon as the Board got into office it set up a pension scheme for itself. One of its innovations was the pooling of all milk. The required pool prices varied from 12 ¾ d. to 14 ¾ d. per gallon. There was a considerable amount of milk which went for manufacturing. Glaxo took a great deal from this parish and it was always a lower price than was liquid milk which went for human consumption. These different prices were then pooled and all producers received the same, though during those first years and up to the War the price was nearly always below a shilling a gallon.

The Board brought stability to the marketing of milk and negotiated with the dairy companies. They were also responsible for payment and the producer got his money promptly every month. Producer retailers were also involved in the scheme and had to be licensed. They had also to make returns at the end of every month. To quote the Board: 'We are now in the position of being able to get rid of that old enemy, undercutting'.

Up to then any one with a few cows could 'hawk' his milk from door to door round the villages and towns. It was taken round in a horse-drawn float in milk cans and measured out into the householder's own jugs or cans. There was a great deal of undercutting, as competition was keen. This method of selling milk often helped the man with just a few cows to keep out of the bankruptcy court. Some of them had been selling butter which at that time was a very poor price. It takes around 3 gallons of milk to make one pound of butter, depending on the type of cow being used.

Selling the milk direct to the customer was a better paying proposition. The Board's scheme soon forced the small producer-retailer out of business. As the form-filling increased, they dropped out. The farmer or cow keeper who sold milk at the door in this village to anyone who cared to fetch it had to be registered with the Board. Most of them decided it wasn't worth it and the large dairy firms took over. The milk was taken twenty miles or so to the nearest depot, then brought back to the countryside where it was originally produced. That situation still applies today with the Milk Marketing Board still going strong.

A case comes to mind where one man in this village milked a few cows and took the milk to his customers in a can. With the coming of the Board and the producer-retailer levy on his sales, he decided he would get out of the milk business. His few cows were sold and as the place was his own, he just sold the grass as a standing crop, if he felt like it. As he was a bachelor with only himself to consider, he lived the life of an eccentric. This was said by some people to have been caused by the Board and its levy. This may not have been quite true as when he bought the place he had some strange ideas. Maybe he just needed that final shove from the Board.

In the 1930s many farmers went into milk, even some on the Wolds where the district had always been considered unsuitable for milk producing. One man took his milk five miles every morning to catch the 6.45 am lorry into Hull at Hutton crossroads. There was not a great deal of profit in it but it was far better than growing corn or feeding bullocks.

At that time most of the milk came off small farms with small herds. Some had only a set of buildings and a bit of grass. There was no arable land needed as cow feed could be bought below the cost of production. It was often said that milking cows seven days a week without a break was slavery. This was quite true as milking machines were in their infancy, not very efficient and the majority of cows were hand milked. We have heard a great deal recently about the Jarrow marchers and what they went through. Yet we never hear anything about those who worked those long hours on the farms and in the villages, for about the same as a man from Jarrow would receive in dole payments. Sometimes it was less, as some of them lived on under £1 a week. Still, if he was his own boss, there were compensations.

There was still a bit of profit to be made out of sheep by buying oldish ewes in Autumn at 30s each, sometimes less. If they had one or two lambs which made £2 each at the market for the summer holiday trade, they made a bit of money, not a great deal but a welcome change when most other ventures were unprofitable. If the ewes were in good condition they went for mutton before the end of the year, and another lot was bought in. This was called keeping a 'flying flock'. In this transaction there had to be a loser and he was the unfortunate seller of the ewes.

The Pig Marketing Board commenced operations on 1 November 1933. The Government were not going to fork out any money if they could help it. They just set up a few Boards instead. Contracts were to be made between the producer, the Pig Marketing Board and the bacon curer. The producer was under an obligation to supply a specified number of pigs with a margin of 10% either way. If he didn't deliver the number of pigs, subject to the 10% either way, he had to pay £1 per pig and any damage which the curer may have incurred. Only a couple of years after the inception of this scheme pigs were making a better price on the open market. Many producers sent them there instead of fulfilling their contracts. The representatives of the board visited their erring producers to pesuade them to honour their contracts. In fairness to them they were not wielding a big stick. As one of them said, if they enforced the penalty of £1 per pig, plus damages to the curers, it would mean the bankruptcy court for many of their suppliers. What kept some of them from honouring their agreement was the fact that they had to take their pigs several miles to the nearest railway station. The LNER had the contract for transporting them. They had also to be within a certain weight, and if above or below there were penalties. Many who had contracted with the Board were not used to weighing pigs; guessing the weight of an animal was more in their line. The nearest thing to weighing any of them ever got was to put the pig in a strong corn bag, 'seck bag'. This wasn't easy with one weighing 12 stones or over. It was then put on an ordinary corn weigh. This was also easier said than done. Still, it showed whether a pig could be kept a bit longer or sent to the bacon factory as soon as possible. The Milk Marketing Board controlled all milk supplies, while the Pig Marketing Board suppliers had an alternative market where prices were nearly always higher. The Board went out of business before the Second World War.

Poultry flocks also increased and the intensive system was coming in. Large huts were built and the hens kept inside. This was a great advantage during the winter months. In 1934 a wood hut specially made for poultry, with inside nest boxes, etc., could be bought from Thornbers of Mytholmroyd, West Yorkshire, for £36.15s.0d. carriage paid. It was 40ft long by 12ft wide and 8ft to the ridge. Walls, roof and floor were made of one-inch boards and it was designed for intensive or semi-intensive use. What such a hut would cost today is anyone's guess.

The poultry expansion was due mainly to the cheap imported food available. Eggs were sometimes as low as 8d. per dozen. There wasn't much profit in them but here again it was ready cash. The industry became more scientific and breeds of hens were improved a great deal. At one time they scratched round in the stackyard, 'staggarth', were a mixture of many breeds, and laid eggs in stacks or hedge bottoms. Now the White or Black Leghorn, or a first cross, was replacing them. Where they were once kept for the wives' pocket money, or to be more accurate, to help pay for some of the household expenses, poultry keeping was now commercialised. Large units of thousands of birds sprang up all over the country. Some of these turned out nothing but day-old chicks. One firm supplying them to egg producers had been started by one man hatching a few eggs under hens. He gave up his job as a miner and concentrated on enlarging the hatchery side and never looked back. Even in those days there were a few success stories. Yet a few years later, due to wartime rationing, most hatcheries were practically closed down.

The farm worker's wage in the 1930s was on the same level as in the preceding decade. In 1933 their numbers had increased for the first time since 1924. In 1934 the building of Driffield and Leconfield aerodromes began and this took up quite a bit of surplus labour at one shilling an hour, as against the farm worker's ninepence. The joiners and other tradesmen who had gone tramp threshing during the winter months or had been on the dole, now had full employment. I think it is true to say that the man who solved the unemployment problem of this country at that time was Hitler. The aerodromes also required a fair amount of permanent staff, most of it local labour. Conditions were slightly better for the rural worker, but farming was still a depressed industry. Not long before the war started Chamberlain, then Prime Minister, was asked what he was going to do about agriculture as war seemed imminent. He said he saw no reason to prepare for something which might never happen. The next year he got what he deserved and was thrown out of office.

In 1939 in Hutton Cranswick there were:

1 cobbler
1 blacksmith
1 butcher
1 saddler
1 bricklayer
1 joiner
1 miller
3 grocers and general stores
2 carriers
1 cycle shop
1 fish shop
1 Post Office at Cranswick
1 Post Office at Hutton

The population of the parish in 1931 was 951 with 333 occupied dwellings. This was the last census until 1951.

The multiple stores in the towns were still selling made-to-measure suits at 30s and 50s. An extra good one cost five pounds and top quality overcoats were about £2. A shirt was 2s to 5s. The quality of the suits was far above those of today. Boots or shoes were from 12s.6d. to £1. A watch could be bought for 5s. and usually kept good time for several years. If it began to go wrong you threw it away and got another one. Prices were never as low again and when war came in September 1939 they crept up gradually.

Orchard Lane, Hutton, c. 1905.

The former village green, Hutton, looking south

Horse Show, Cranswick.

Feast 1911, Cranswick Green.

Soldiers and families 1920.

Charles Watson, builder of Cranswick School 1874

Hutton Cranswick Show Committee in the 1940s.

Jim Walker, Foreman at South Hall until 1921, breaking horses.

Mr. Morris at Burn Butts, with Tom Sissons of Fair View in background.

161

V.E.Day, 1946.

A School group at Cranswick, c. 1900.

162

Mr Wethrell and boys of Hutton Road School late 19th Century.

The Cenotaph on Cranswick Green on Remembrance Day in 1920s.

CHAPTER TWENTY-THREE

THE SECOND WORLD WAR

When war was declared on that first Sunday in September it came as a shock to most people. Still, they were all sick of Hitler's raving. (As one man said, 'He disn't hafe mak d'ord wireless ring'.) Even the most peaceable citizen thought the time had come to put a spoke in his wheel. After all the threatenings from Germany, everybody expected a mass air raid with gas and everything else horrible that could be used. When there was an air raid warning it helped to show how un-prepared we were. This raid was a false alarm due to some planes being wrongly identified and was the start of the phoney war which lasted all the winter.

The Government issued exhortations to the farmers asking them to get the corn harvested as soon as possible, which was a bit daft as all the corn was wet and sodden. This was the first time for nearly twenty years that any Government had ever bothered what happened to the harvest. The War Agricultural Executive Committee, henceforth always known as the War Ag., was formed. Their representatives were sent to visit every holding, almost like a burglar 'casing the joint', to see what the occupier's cropping plans were and whether any grass could be ploughed out. At last the politicians were forced to recognize the value of agriculture as so many of those cheap imports of grain, etc., were sent to the bottom of the sea by the submarines.

After nine fairly mild winters, that of 1939-40 was one of the most severe most people could remember. Branches of trees were killed by the severe frost and just dropped off. The water works on Southburn Road broke down and were out of action for several days. The mains system had been installed not long before war was declared. That was just long enough for most of the pumps to 'seize up'. There were a few still working where water could be obtained for making tea. For other purposes it was a case of bashing a way through the ice of the nearest pond. For a while we turned the clock back and lived like our ancestors. The following winter was just as bad. The next was just a little milder. During one of those winters a passenger train got stuck all night in a snow drift in the cutting near Hutton gates. This severe winter weather made life harder as people required more fuel. Stock also required more feed, as they had to be kept longer indoors.

With the outbreak of war, children, and in some cases whole families, were dumped in inadequate premises in the villages, or anywhere in the country. In this village a good number of houses in Southgate were condemned by the local authority in the summer of 1939. Not long after they were filled with evacuees. Most of these were very poor. One woman had pawned her shoes before leaving Hull. On the whole they were well treated by those who took them in. Most of them were better fed than they had ever been before. But it was as if they had been transported to a foreign land and when nothing happened in the first few weeks of the war, nearly all of them drifted back to the towns. A few of the children stayed permanently.

Building the Cranswick aerodrome began in 1940. This also made employment for local men. The phoney war ended when Hitler attacked France, Belgium and Holland in May 1940. When France capitulated, the bombing of this country really started. Most nights the German bombers were attacking different places in East Yorkshire. The city of Hull and Driffield aerodrome were targets and bombs were dropped haphazardly on isolated places. This was sometimes referred to as 'Auld Hitler dropping is muck again'. It was a case of working all day and fire-watching at night.

What no one wanted was a clear night with what was called a 'bomber's moon'. A misty night gave welcome relief to the civilian population. During those summer nights of 1940 the Germans sometimes had huge flares hung like chandeliers in the sky to act as markers and guide their planes when they crossed the coast. These lit up the heavens and the ordinary individual looking up at them from the ground wondered why the British fighter planes couldn't get up and shoot them down.

Goering decided that the aerodromes would have to be put out of action and in August the daylight raids began. In that month Driffield aerodrome was attacked about midday one day. A few planes were destroyed on the ground, some people killed and a good deal of damage done to the hangars. The German planes had no fighter cover and they lost quite a few planes themselves. Some were seen limping back to the coast and looked as though they would never reach the Fatherland. There was an unofficial report that some of the returning German planes met a number of British fighter bombers homeward bound from a raid on occupied Denmark and lost a few planes in an action over the sea.

Ever since the beginning of the war a strict censorship had been imposed. This also included the weather. If there had been any bombs dropped in this area, all the news bulletins said was 'Enemy activity in the North East'. The German radio was more specific. William Joyce, Lord Haw Haw, announced with great relish that 'The Luftwaffe had dropped bombs of the heaviest calibre on certain places. Hull was one of these'. After the War, Joyce, who had tried to dodge the issue by claiming he wasn't a British citizen, was also dropped - at the end of a rope. Lord Haw Haw's propaganda didn't have much effect. In fact it put ordinary people's backs up.

Before the end of 1940, except for a few sneak day-time raiders, the Germans reverted to night-time bombing. This continued through the winter until May 1941 when the Germans prepared to attack Russia. A fire-watching system was organised with a post, later equipped with a siren, at Cranswick. This was connected by telephone to the one at Mr A Southwick's house (now Mr Blackburn's) at Hutton. Later, on the instigation of the Vicar, the Rev. George Storer, this was removed to the vicarage and a rota established.

The Vicar, with the best of motives, like many of his predecessors, acted as though nothing would get done unless he organised it. He sometimes arranged unofficial fire-fighting exercises and was rather aggrieved when some of the fire watchers didn't turn up. He didn't seem to realise that they were working all day and were sometimes up most of the night protecting theirs and other people's property, stock and crops when there was an air raid. When daylight came the Vicar could go to bed. After having a telling-off by at least one of the fire watchers he said no more about trying to get some of them into the Army. During the later years of the war a few women were enrolled as messengers to assist the fire fighters. They were all fully fitted with uniform, but were never needed. When the war was over they received an official letter of thanks and were allowed to keep their uniforms. The poor old fire watcher who had borne the brunt during the war years didn't even get thanked. He was allowed to keep his tin hat, which could always serve a useful purpose if put underneath the bed!

After a winter of sporadic bombing when the air raid warning was sounded nearly every night and Hull took a battering, spring had nearly arrived when, on 19th March 1941, Goering's bombers made a determined attack on Hull and the surrounding district. This village was now in the front line as Cranswick Aerodrome was practically completed. Not much more than a mile away as the crow flies, there was a huge bomb dump which, if it had ever gone up, would have taken a large chunk of East Yorkshire with it. Driffield aerodrome was about the same distance away and was often a target. Now it was almost always attacked at night. The raids on 19th March started in Hull about eleven o'clock. From near the old Hutton Mill, whole plane-loads of incendiary bombs could be seen dropping in the Hull area interspersed with high explosives. Like a creeping barrage these could be seen moving away from Hull in this direction. Slowly they moved across the carrs until they arrived here in the early hours of the morning. The incendiaries whistled overhead like a covey of partridges in full flight. Then they could be heard plopping as they hit the roadway. Many dropped on soft ground in the fields where they did no danger. Some were ploughed up years after in a corroded condition. Water only made these incendiaries burn brighter. It was seldom that they were accommodating enough to drop where there was a heap of sand. Soil was the next best thing; cow muck was also used. Just over the parish boundary Watton Abbey Farm had seventy high explosive bombs dropped indiscriminately over the fields as well as incendiaries. Some of them started a small stack fire. The pilots of the German planes must have thought this fire denoted a place of strategic importance and this was thought to be the reason for the bombs dropped on and around Hutton Cranswick. Most of the bomb aiming was very bad and it was just luck if they hit anything.

In Cranswick Mrs Arnell's grocer's shop was damaged beyond repair. There was also a certain amount of blast damage to buildings. Hutton church was set on fire by an incendiary bomb towards the end of the raid, about three o'clock in the morning. Some of the pews were smouldering, and it was impossible to get inside, but by smashing a window and directing a stirrup pump hose pipe on to the blaze, the local fire fighters averted what could have been a serious calamity. When the Driffield Fire Brigade arrived later, the danger was past. That stirrup pump was the only one they had, though to their advantage there was a huge tub of rain water in the right place. After that there were always several pumps kept ready for emergencies. It has often been speculated what might have happened if the Church had really got ablaze. On the hilltop it would have been like a giant beacon, as the Germans were dropping bombs anywhere where they saw a blaze, although most of the planes were heading for home. Even though the German bombing was haphazard, with a big church fire they might have caused a great deal more damage and loss of life.

At Highfield Farm the house was nearly obliterated and the Severs family, father, mother and two school-children, were killed when a land mine exploded near the front door. A lad in his teens who worked there and lived in with the family had a miraculous escape. He went home the night before, decided to stay and go back the next morning. Two horses in a stable at the far side of the foldyard escaped without a scratch. That farm was ill-fated, as a year later a Wellington bomber scraped alongside the farm buildings and belly-flopped in a field near the house, as did another one not long after the house was bombed.

When daybreak came the damage was not as great as expected, as most of the high explosive bombs had dropped in the fields. Some hadn't exploded. There were odd small house fires, but these were soon attended to. All this must have been intended for Hull, and I believe Haw Haw said so on the radio. If all those bombs had really dropped on Hull instead of the low wet carr lands, as many of them did, there would have been a great deal more damage and loss of life. The last of the incendiaries dropped to the north west of Hutton, just beyond the Hull to Driffield road. There were just a few dropped near the outskirts of Driffield. Yet a male telephone operator there got a medal for sticking to his post when most of the bombs were dropped three miles away.

During the raids on the Liverpool area, the German planes often crossed the coast here. On their way back they dropped the odd bomb or two. These may have been some which they had been unable to release on the target and were just dumped anywhere. There were a few more raids on this district, mainly on Hull, in May, after which the Nazis were fully engaged in Russia and there were more quiet nights than most people had enjoyed for nearly two years. Not long before the end of the war, a flying bomb which must have been launched from a plane went rattling across in the general direction of Liverpool. After five and a half years of war in Europe, that was the end of the bombing.

During those years there were many rumours, partly due to the strict censorship imposed. There were frequent warnings from the Government about careless talk. In 1940 identity cards were issued and the public were asked to keep a look-out for parachutists, as they were then called, who could be dropped at night over England. One rumour was that some of these had established themselves in a Sunderlandwick wood. People who spread rumours are always quite sure they are true, though this one could be easily discounted by the fact that there were Army and Air Force bases only a mile or two away, and they would hardly allow a small group of Nazis to survive for long. This fear of parachutists arose from the facts reported in the newspapers that Germans had been dropped from planes wearing Dutch Army uniforms during the invasion of Holland. As a matter of fact, there were very few who landed on English soil in this manner and they were on espionage missions.

In the summer of 1940 an invasion by Hitler was expected and the Local Defence Volunteers, later called the Home Guard, were formed. Like the Civil Defence, they trained in their spare time and were always ready for any emergency. The civilian population were behind Churchill when he said 'Should the invaders come there will be no lying down of the people in submission as we have seen in other countries. We shall defend every village, town and city'.

As the war went on the Italian and then German prisoners came to work in the fields. As the troops moved out of the camps across to Europe, they moved in. The camp in Hobman Lane housed those who worked in this parish and in the surrounding district. Most of them had returned by 1948. They were a far different lot from those who had marched arrogantly across Europe when Hitler was in his heyday, and had screamed about marching against England. Some of them had been in the Luftwaffe when it had dropped bombs on England. It was said by some of the local residents that they should be made to fill in all the bomb craters they had made round here, which no doubt some of them had to do in the ordinary course of their work on the farms.

As the war dragged on, rationing was introduced. Pig Clubs were formed and pigs were kept in all kinds of places and by all sorts of people. A Driffield doctor with a patient who was a Cranswick farmer got corn from him on the side to eke out his pig ration. The Pig Clubs were allowed a small amount of meal for each member who was feeding a pig for bacon. Public Health regulations were ignored. Even the most fastidious individual would rather put up with a few stinks than go hungry.

There were strict controls on pig killing, which had to be done by licence as all meat was strictly rationed. In spite of this there was a black market, as there were always people prepared to pay much more than the market price.

Eggs also practically disappeared from the shops. Here again there were individuals seeking eggs outside the normal channels. Most of the large egg producers had closed down as poultry feeding stuffs were severely rationed. Nearly all the few eggs available came from the farms where there was always a supply of small or damaged corn. In effect the clock was turned back to the time when poultry scratched round the stacks for a living. One farmer who lived near Cranswick village was selling wheat out of the stoock for poultry feed. This was during the wet harvest of 1944 when all the heads were grown together in a green mass, or 'all uv a attrill' as it was more often called.

There was one case reported in a farming journal of a man who before the war had kept poultry on a large scale. He was trying to supplement his meagre poultry rations by mixing in finely shredded paper. There is no record of what results he achieved. His hens may have been conscripted by the Government to churn out paper for the ever-increasing quantity of forms required by various departments. Millers and feed merchants were selling damaged and blackened wheat from bombed and burnt-out mills for poultry feed, some of it nearly cinders, and the price was higher than what the grower was receiving for good wheat off the farm. Bread was not rationed until 1946 when the war was over. The millers who before the war didn't want to use British wheat could now mix barley and potatoes in it. The War Ag. brought the first combines into this parish, though it was predicted by nearly everybody connected with farming that they had no future. The same thing had been said about the tractors when used by the Government to plough some land adjoining Corpslanding Road during the First World War.

From 1939 onwards, tractors began to be used in increasing numbers, subject to the severe wartime restrictions. The horses couldn't compete with the tractors in tearing up all the neglected acres. One argument in favour of tractors was that they didn't eat when they weren't working. The horseman might argue that his horses could live on home-grown food and didn't need imported fuel which had to be brought across the sea at the cost of men's lives.

The Women's Land Army was formed again and they tackled all kinds of jobs.

Private cars were off the road unless their owners could prove they were being used for essential purposes. Posters appeared with the words 'Is your journey really necessary?'. Motorists were often stopped by police. One dodge used by some farmers who wanted a night out was to have a trailer hitched to the car with a calf or a bit of straw in it.

With the end of the war, the fields of this parish had lost that neglected look which had hung over them for nearly twenty years. All over England the countryside smiled again, with its hedges in reasonable condition and once derelict land growing crops of corn. There were still weedy crops to be seen, but spraying, that eliminator of so much drudgery, was being developed and by the 1950s a crop of corn full of rubbish was very rarely seen. If there had been no World War Two, would agriculture have remained in its depressed state? If it had been left to the politicians to decide, it almost certainly would.

CHAPTER TWENTY-FOUR

POST - WAR CHANGES

After the war most farmers expected to be thrown aside just as they had been sacrificed for cheap imports in 1921. Some talked about a return to "dog and stick" farming. This was letting land sow itself down to grass, keeping a few livestock on it and living as cheaply as possible. But this time there was a difference. The country had no money. It had all gone in the war years. The British Empire was crumbling and the cheap imports from it, which had ruined the pre- war agricultural industry, were no more. It was a case of using our own resources.

A system was introduced whereby deficiency payments were made when the market fell below the guaranteed one fixed by the government, which more or less gave stability. Often the guaranteed price was never reached as the Government had a scheme, as in the case of cereals, where if a certain amount overall was produced, the price came down. This system of deficiency payments remained until this country joined the EEC. It was often attacked as "feather bedding" farmers. Yet it was often forgotten that the price of wheat had remained the same for twenty years while the price of bread had been steadily rising. One of these critics was a member of the Labour Government called Evans. He was a minor official in the Ministry of Agriculture and acquired the name of "Feather bed" Evans. As that same Government was the architect of the scheme he criticised so much, his remarks were an embarrassment to it and he was kicked out.

The first post-war Minister of Agriculture was Tom Williams and he remained in office until 1951 when the Labour Government was defeated. He was held in great esteem by everyone whatever their politics. Many in the agricultural industry would have liked him to remain in office.

During the war, animal feeding stuff prices were subsidised by the Government. When the subsidies were taken off after the war the prices were doubled. Where most of them had been kept at pre war level, they had now jumped to £15 per ton. (At the present day some compounds are £140 per ton) For nearly thirty years after the war barley and wheat usually averaged about £23 per ton. Grain prices remained more or less stable until 1973 when the Russians bought all Americas surplus wheat. This had the effect of doubling the price of English grain. Since then barley has averaged £70 to £90 per ton and wheat £80 - £90.

Threshing and baling was £11 per day labour excluded. At the present time a threshing day with labour included would cost in the region of

£250. The three sets, which travelled the Hutton Cranswick area for many years, are now consigned to the scrap heap. Some threshing machines, those symbols of hard work and dust are preserved to give demonstrations at steam rallies. No one who worked with them is sorry to see them go, yet for well over 100 years they were part of the farming scene and gave employment to many during the winter months just like the flail which preceded them. The last threshing in this parish was about 10 to 15 years ago. Now the combine has taken over completely.

"Muck plugging", when all the muck from the fold yards or other buildings had to be man handled by forks, has gone. There are no regrets on that account. It meant a lot of sweat and often blistered hands, yet it was a quick way of getting warmed up on a cold and frosty morning. But a great deal of "muck plugging" was also done in the warm days of summer. That was when the fold yards were empty and the stock turned out to grass.

Continuous corn growing a thing unheard of by our ancestors has been popular for a number of years. This was once said to be the shortest way to the bankruptcy court. Ordinary agricultural land is now being sold for over £2000 an acre.

CHAPTER TWENTY-FIVE

HUTTON CRANSWICK HORSE, FOAL AND HORTICULTURAL SOCIETY
(Or 'Cranswick Show')

Most of the people who attended the Show called it 'Cransick' not Cranswick, and before Show Day, you could hear people ask: 'Is tha gooin ti Cransick Show?'

The Minute Books in the possession of Mr J. Thompson of South Hall, Cranswick, date from 27 April 1911. Yet there must have been a Show at the end of the last century because when Mr G. Rayner, the Secretary, retired in 1920, he had held the post for twenty-one years. At this first meeting recorded in the Minutes of April 1911 were:

Chairman:	W.P. Kirby, Cranswick Common
ViceChairman:	A.W. Simpson, Throstle Nest
	W. Morriss, Cranswick
	G. Hobson, Sheepman Farm, Cranswick
	J. Holtby, Rotsea
	J. Catton, South Hall
	J. Morriss, Cranswick
	D. Robson, Cranswick
	H. Atkinson, Hutton
	J. Robson, Cranswick
	A. Dossor, Cranswick

The Minutes of the last meeting were read and approved so there are some Minute Books missing. Mr G. Rayner was the former village school headmaster and had only recently retired. He was a remarkable penman and his writing was good copperplate. He got £4 a year for his services and his deputy, J. Robson, £1.

One of the Show Committee, G. Hobson, served on that body more or less continuously until the demise of the Show and Sports in 1957. Those early shows were held in a field nearly opposite Megginson Lane End. Later, they were held in one belonging to South Hall at the bottom end of Southgate. It is still called Show Field. In that year, 1911, Sir Luke White of Driffield, was elected President. Only two months later he sent a guinea and suggested that Sir Prince Smith of Southburn should be invited to take the post instead of him. The Secretary said Sir Prince had been asked before but had been unable to accept - a diplomatic way of saying he didn't want the job.

At the 1911 show there were prizes for the best pair of horses in plough gearing driven in the ring. 'Plough gearing' meant collars, blinders and backhand tracers. 1st Prize £2; 2nd Prize £1. There were also prizes for farm servants with the cleanest horse gearing: 1st Prize 5s; 2nd Prize 2s.6d. The Driffield Territorial Band was engaged to play on the Show Field. The sports were held in the evening when there were ten events. One of these was the quarter-mile handicap race. Mr G. Hobson promised a greasy pig to be competed for if the event was legal. Mr J. Holtby was to enquire into its legality, but the matter of the greasy pig never came up again. A dance was held in the Foresters Hall in the evening.

The next year a Miss Byas of Driffield was given £1.1s.0d. as the best lady driver at the Show held the previous year. A Mr Pierone was to have the sole right to sell ice-cream at the Show, for which he paid 10s. The Show Committee also gave the job of bellman to Mr R. Briggs. He was also the postman. His job was to ring a handbell to attract people's attention and then announce the various events. This he did for many years. Mr G. Simpson of George Street, Driffield, was re-elected veterinary surgeon. His premises are now a motor accessory shop.

In 1913 the Committee passed a resolution that the charge for admission to the Show Field should be 1s. This may not seem much by present-day standards, but it must be remembered that most of the local people attending the Show were only earning 2s.6d. per day. The Secretary's salary was increased to £5 and that of his assistants to £3.

A new class was introduced in 1914, namely, for the best cottager's cow in calf or milk. 1st Prize £2; 2nd Prize £1. At this time there were nearly forty lane cows, all, or nearly all, the property of the cottages of Hutton and Cranswick. The Show Committee must have thought there would be some rowdy elements attending the Show as they engaged five policemen to keep order. In later years there were only three. This, the last of the pre-First World War Shows was held in the last week of July. War was declared on 4 August.

There were no more Shows until 1921, though the Committee met at intervals. At one of these meetings, 17 February 1919, A.W. Consitt and A.W. Simpson were delegated to represent the Society at the funeral of Sir Mark Sykes at Sledmere. On 1 March 1920 Mr G. Rayner resigned as Secretary after holding that post for twenty-one years. Mr E. Morriss was elected in his stead. Two months later Mr Rayner was made a present of £2 in recognition of the great services he had rendered to the Society.

In 1921 there was a full-scale Show and Sports. This was probably one of the best of the Cranswick Shows. The agricultural industry was in better shape than ever before. There was a bit more money in everybody's pocket, though the depression was just around the corner. That year was also one of the finest and driest on record. This Show was held on the last Friday in July, and many farmers attending it were going to start harvesting the following Monday. Most of the corn was in the stack before the end of August.

The 1922 Show was held on 21 July. There was a class for farmer's hacks, 1st Prize £2.2s.0d; 2nd Prize £1; 3rd Prize 10s. Motor cars were beginning to be used and the hackneys were declining in numbers. In the nineteenth century and into the early part of this one, Moores of Burn Butts and Buttles of Kirkburn were noted hackney breeders. There was also a class for Clydesdales three years old and upwards, 1st Prize £3, 2nd Prize £2, 3rd Prize £1. G. Good who at the time, along with his partner, C. Hodgson, farmed South Hall gave the first prize.

At the Sports in the evening there were flat races of varying distance from the quarter-mile to eighty yards for boys. There was also an eighty-yard race for girls, a one-mile cycle race and a musical chairs on cycle race. There was one pony variety race where the contestants had to 'ride once round the ring, dismount and put on a blouse and skirt. Remount, ride round the ring; take an apple from a bucket of water with the mouth; remount and ride round the ring. Dismount and light a cigarette. Remount and ride to winning post with cigarette lighted. A hurdle to be jumped each time round the ring. Any omission disqualifies the rider.'

There is no mention of what the winners received in the way of prizes. For an ordinary pony variety race they were 1st, £2; 2nd, £1 and 3rd, 10s.

The Minute Books from 4 December 1922 until 1933 are missing, though there had been Show and Sports meetings in those years. Due to the depression the Show dwindled, but the Sports flourished. The Committee must have been at loggerheads with their Chairman, Mr G. Hobson, as on 24 October 1933 a letter was read by the Clerk and signed by all the members expressing no confidence in him. This was due to his recent actions, which the Committee thought were not in the best interests of the Society.

In 1934 there was no Show held, only the Evening Sports when there were the usual flat races, horse races, etc. The following year the Society was beginning to feel the effects of the depression, as two of the Committee members wished to have the Sports cancelled. They were outvoted and the decision was to carry on as usual. Two other members wished to have Cranswick Band engaged to play during the Sports, but it was decided to have no band at all. The Secretary, Mr E. Morriss, was paid £16 for his services but he gave £8 back to the Society.

There was a balance of £77.19s.11d. In the bank for the year 1936, as against £38.13s.8d. the year before. So prospects were a little brighter. Cranswick Band's tender of £2.10s.0d. for playing at the Sports was not accepted. The £4.10s.0d. one of BOCM was. Why the Cranswick band being a local one, wasn't engaged to play isn't mentioned in the Minutes. This wasn't the first time it had been turned down and the higher tender of a band from outside accepted. Maybe some of the Show Committee doubted the musical abilities of the Cranswick Band.

The 1937 Show was mainly horticultural though there were classes for the best ears of corn. This was held in the Foresters Hall on 7 August. The following year there was again the tussle between the supporters of Cranswick Band and BOCM, which the latter won. (BOCM British Oil and Cake Mills, a Hull firm whose band played at many local functions in the East Riding.)

There was no Show or Sports during the war years. In early 1946 the Show and Sports Committee made plans for a full size Show with horse, cattle, fruit and vegetable classes. There were also decorated horse classes as well as horses in plough gearing and driven in strings. In the evening a larger Sports Meeting than ever was to be held with a dance to follow in the Foresters Hall. As after the First World War, history was repeating itself in that agriculture was out of the doldrums and this helped to make this show a success. In April 1947 the Show Committee had £316 in the bank. The next year reserves had increased to £459. There was never any record in the Minutes of the attendance at the various Show and Sports events, just a statement of cash in the bank.

By the end of 1948 post-war enthusiasm was waning and the Show was going downhill. In 1949 it was mainly horticultural and the events for Saturday 23 July were mainly for children. Most of these were pony races and fancy dress on ponies. Sports were held in the evening.

By 1950 the Society's capital was shrinking and the balance in hand was £328.1s.5d. In 1951 the Show had classes for agricultural horses, cows and heifers in milk. 1952 saw the last of the agricultural shows proper when the classes were the same as the year before. At this time there were very few horses left on the farms in the parish. On 20 November of that year the Committee must have felt the need of some good cheer as it was proposed that they had a dinner at Miss Atkinson's Guest House, Driffield, at a cost of 10s. each.

J. Thompson and R. Milner were appointed Joint Secretaries on 24 May 1954 in place of Mr E. Morriss who had held the post for thirty-four years. At the same meeting it was resolved that the Agricultural Show be discontinued for the time being, but that every effort be made to continue the Society. The Sports were held on the evening of 22nd. July, commencing at four o'clock. Here is the programme of events in detail:

80 yards flat race for boys 59: 1st. 10s; 2nd., 5s; 3rd., 2s.6d.

Ditto for girls (same ages and prizes).

80 yards for boys 10.14 years: 1st. 10s; 2nd., 5s; 3rd., 2s.6d.

Ditto for girls (prizes the same).

Pony jumping, not exceeding 12.2 hands. Rider not exceeding 16 years: 1st, £3; 2nd, £2; 3rd. £1.

Open jumping 1st, £8; 2nd £5; 3rd. £3.

Variety race (open): 1st, £2, 2nd. £1; 3rd. 10s.

South Hall Derby run at 6 o'clock: 1st. £15; 2nd., £8; 3rd., £3.

Motor cycle race (heats): 1st. £15; 2nd., £10; 3rd., £3.

Kilnwick Stakes: 1st. £10; 2nd., £5; 3rd., £3.

Motor cycle race (final): 1st. £3; 2nd., £2; 3rd., £1.

Musical chairs (open): 1st. £2; 2nd., £1; 3rd., 10s.

Cranswick St Leger: 1st. £20; 2nd., £10; 3rd., £5.

Motor cycle race (heats): 1st. 15s; 2nd., 10s; 3rd., 5s.

Potato race on horseback (open): 1st. £2; 2nd., £1; 3rd., 10s.

Event 16, Motor cycle final: No entries.

Abbey Stakes: 1st. £8; 2nd., £5; 3rd., £3.

All of these horse races, the South Hall Derby and the others, were first run when the Show and Sports started up again after the First World War. They were always very popular and attracted many bookmakers in spite of the notice in the Show field that 'Betting is strictly prohibited'.

The last of the Sports Meetings was held in 1957, but entries were very low and there was clearly no point in carrying on any longer. So after nearly fifty years or it may have been far longer the Hutton Cranswick Horse, Foal and Horticultural Society or 'Cranswick Show and Sports' as it was better known, came to the end of its days. It had been near death many times due to wars, depressions and other causes, but there were always a few enthusiasts determined to keep it going. There were many East Riding Village Shows in this century. Most of them have gone, but I think it is safe to say that 'Cransick' show and Sports took pride of place among them.

CHAPTER TWENTY-SIX

VILLAGE FAMILIES

There are so many families who have been part of Hutton Cranswick for centuries and we can consider only a few of them here. Some of their ancestors will have lived here long before there were any records. Unlike the Hothams and the Londesboroughs, their deeds were never chronicled. They were mainly tradesmen and craftsmen.

Such a one was Robert Allethorpe, clockmaker, of Hutton Cranswick, though his name is in no trade directory. As far as can be ascertained, he lived at Hutton from about 1760 to 1780. He had left the village before the end of the century. One of the grandfather clocks he made two hundred years ago is still going; it only loses time slightly. The Hutton couple who own it say it has been in their family for three generations, perhaps far longer. Robert Allethorpe may have been dead for nearly 200 years, but his clock still ticks on, a monument to his craftsmanship.

The farmers of Hutton Cranswick parish seem to have moved around, but not the joiners, the cobblers, the tailors and the blacksmiths; their occupations kept them in the village and business came to them. There they developed roots, in fact, they were the village. They helped to make it and contributed much to its development. Often, son followed father into the trade, whatever it may have been. This makes them easier to trace. Some of these names still survive, though the village trades associated with them died out after the First World War.

THE BARKERS

The first one, William, came from Bridlington in the early part of the nineteenth century and lived in a house in Back Street (Orchard Lane), Hutton, nearly opposite the Methodist Chapel. His wife was born at Cranswick in the latter part of the eighteenth century. There were two Jesse Barkers, son and grandson of William, and they were both shoemakers and sextons. Jesse the younger also kept livestock and had a certain amount of land. He lived at what was the shop and Post Office in Front Street, Hutton. His wife ran the shop and she got the GPO to set up a Post Office by collecting signatures from the local people. Tragically, her husband Jesse was killed in an accident in 1924 on the Driffield to Hutton Road. The name has gone but their direct descendants are still living here.

BOWES, Blacksmiths

The first Bowes to be recorded as a blacksmith was William, who was born at Hutton Cranswick in 1783. In 1851 he had a blacksmiths shop at the lower end of Main Street, Cranswick. Later the business was carried on for many years at the premises opposite the WI Hall. When the last of the Bowes blacksmiths, Ted, died in 1936, the business was taken over by E. Davison, later by C. Eling but the business was then declining. E. Davison did a bit of horse shoeing and odd jobs at the old prisoner of war camp in Hobman Lane until the 1950s when he sold out and went to Bridlington. He was the last of the old time blacksmiths as all the agricultural horses had gone and mechanisation demanded different skills. It was also the end of the line for the Bowes family when Ted's daughter, Dorothy, died in 1976.

DAVID CONSITT, Carrier

David Consitt lived in Southgate and carried on his business from there until he died in the early 1920s. His ancestors were the Stephensons, once yeomen farmers. There was a John Stephenson at the time of the Enclosures who owned a house and small paddock at the bottom end of Southgate and one in Main Street, Cranswick, and also 20 acres of land near Burn Butts. He could have been one of the same family. There are Consitts still living in Cranswick.

THE SANDERSONS

The 1913 trade directory lists Edmund Sanderson, bootmaker; Johnson Sanderson, tailor; William Sanderson, postmaster. They were all of the same stock. Edmund Sanderson's shop was on the end of one of the houses known as Camerton Cottages, Main Street, Cranswick. It was knocked down only recently to make way for house modernisation.

Johnson Sanderson's tailor shop was behind the Green. William Sanderson, postmaster, kept the grocery shop and Post Office in the Main Street, which became the fish shop. He remained there until 1925 when he bought the Manor House, Hutton. He was very much anti-squire and it was he who used to make rude remarks to Fred Reynard when he rode by.

The first Sanderson to reside in Cranswick was an itinerant tailor from Scotland who came first to Sunderlandwick. He stayed there a while and then moved to Cranswick. The first of them to appear in the Parish Register was William a 'taylor', in the seventeenth century. As the years went by there were different offshoots of the family, mostly tailors. Often son followed father in the trade. The last was Ted who died in 1965 and who learnt the trade from his father, James. Like most other village tailors the business ended not long after the First World War.

There were joiners and blacksmiths as well as cobblers and tailors among them. Some were freeholders like Johnson and Samuel Sanderson mentioned earlier. Many of them moved away, but there were always some left to carry on the business. The Sanderson name still survives today.

THE GOWTHORPES

The first Gowthorpe to live in Cranswick was Richard, who was proprietor of the Cross-Keys in the early part of the nineteenth century. The exact date when he came to live there is not quite clear, but he was licensee of the Cross-Keys in 1840. He was born at Cottingham in 1784. One of his sons was a druggist and took over the shop next door. He died quite young, at the age of 26. W. Sanderson married Gowthorpe's daughter and became the owner of the shop, which was later to be the Post Office. Another of the Gowthorpes helped to build the Wesleyan Chapel. Blyth Gowthorpe was once the proprietor of the Board Inn, Front Street, Hutton. Today there are still Gowthorpes living in Hutton.

THE WATSONS

Henry Watson was born at Nafferton in 1813. In 1851 he kept the White Horse, Cranswick. It was then classified as just a beerhouse and Henry was a bricklayer. His son Charles built the school in 1875. Later he took over Jubilee Farm, Hutton, once a public house, the Board Inn. He died in the early 1920s and was followed by his son, also Charles. When he died in 1939 the place was sold. There are no more Watsons, but many of their descendants still live here.

ROBSON SUMMERSON, Joiner

When Robson Summerson, or Rob as he was known, died not long after the First World War, that was the end of the Summersons as joiners and carriers. His brother Frank who died about twenty years ago was the last of the line in Cranswick. George Summerson was a carrier in the early part of the last century, as was Mary a few years later. In 1851 Francis Summerson was a joiner and he was followed by Rob, whose premises were opposite the Cranswick pond. When he died his premises were taken over by Mr R. Wilkinson, saddler. Up to recent years the workshop was the Post Office.

ROBERT WEATHERILL, Roper

The Weatherills' ropery was near Station Lane, Cranswick. The house is now occupied by Mr T. Thompson. On some maps the rope walk is shown. In the 1840 Directory a William Kelsey was a roper. Robert Weatherill of Hutton Cranswick married his daughter and the business became the Weatherills. At one time they did a large trade supplying farmers with halters, sheep nets and ropes. They employed several local men. The last of the Weatherills to be a roper was another Robert. The business closed down shortly after the First World War. The last Weatherill in Hutton Cranswick was Harold, who died in 1973. Previous to the Kelseys and Weatherills, ropers, was William Best, though where he lived is not known.

THE SPINKS

The roots of the Spinks go back into the eighteenth century, perhaps much further. In the middle of the last century there were father and son, both shoemakers. Another was a blacksmith. One of them helped to build the Hull to Bridlington railway. At the beginning of this century Frank Spink had a threshing set of his own and went round the farms. His daughter, Miss Elsie Spink, later Mrs W. Simpson, taught at the Infants School. The last to carry the name is Miss N. Spink. Mr K. Simpson of Hutton, grandson of Frank Spink, still carries on the tradition of the Spink family in that he is a builder, joinery contractor and does a bit of farming as well.

SISSONS, Joiners

Elizabeth Sissons was head of the household after her husband died in the early years of the nineteenth century. She was born at Hutton Cranswick in 1779. Her son Christopher was carrying on the family joinery business, probably following in his father's footsteps. His younger brother George also became a carpenter. The business was carried on from premises next to Megginsons' Grocery Stores. When Mr Tom Sissons died about twenty years ago, the joinery business ended with him. The name still remains in the person of Mr Gordon Sissons.

THE HOBSONS

The Directory of 1840 states that George Hobson was a freeholder. Eleven years later he had ten acres of land and lived at Sheepman Farm, Sheepman Lane, Cranswick. He was born at Hutton Cranswick in 1779. By the beginning of this century the Hobsons owned Little Common Farm and a considerable amount of land which they worked themselves.

Another George Hobson was a Parish Councillor, Rural District Councillor and County Councillor. Some of the land in Sheepman Lane still belongs to the Hobsons who are living in Cranswick.

THE TURNERS

David Turner, cordwainer, was born at Hutton Cranswick in 1788. A cordwainer was a shoemaker but was a bit 'betterma' class than an ordinary cobbler. The James Turner, shoemaker, whose name appears in the 1919 Directory, was the grandson of David Turner the cordwainer. The last of the Turners, cobblers or shoemakers, was Walter, our controversial Parish Councillor, who did his cobbling in a building near Sheepman Lane End. He died not long before the Second World War. The name has gone, but descendants of the Turners still live in Cranswick.

CATTONS of South Hall

The first Catton to occupy South Hall was John, who was born at Stockton-on-Forest, near York, in 1791. He must have come to South Hall on the Driffield to Beverley Road, while quite a young man as his son, also John, was born there in 1823. By 1851 there were over 700 acres attached to the farm. Not long before the First World War it was bought by James Catton. When he retired and sold up in 1921, the farm was let. It was sold to the sitting tenant. Frank, who died recently, was the last of them in the parish. His father, Henry Catton, farmed Gannock, or Manor House Farm, until 1927. His uncle J.Y. Catton farmed Rotsea Manor until 1943. They were both grandsons of the first John Catton.

TIM FLETCHER

He lived in the house in Mill Street, facing Church Lane End. In 1820 there was a fair amount of land attached to the place and John Fletcher farmed it. He must have visited the Board Inn or the two beerhouses in Hutton too often and this was said to be the reason for most of the land being sold. Some was bought by Reynards of Sunderlandwick. Before the First World War Tim Fletcher went to Bridlington market every Saturday with a cart load of garden produce. This ended when the war started. He died in the early 1920s and his grandson and granddaughter still live in his house.

HERBERT PEARSON

He followed his father, William Pearson, into the blacksmith's business. He lived for the greater part of his life in the house in Front Street, Hutton, now a coal depot. Later he lived in the house next door where his mother once lived. The blacksmith's shop still stands on the corner of Front Street, now Church Street. The Parish Council noticeboard now adorns one side of it.

On the end of the building there used to be an old tin Hudson's soap advertisement which had been there most of this century and children going to school used to blast it with stones and make a terrible racket. This made llerbert Pearson stick his head over the half door of the shop and threaten them. When he died in 1936 that was the end of the blacksmith's in Hutton. Sets of harrows with his name on are still around today. When William Pearson first came to Hutton is obscure, but it must have been well over a hundred years ago. There are now no members of the family living in Hutton.

WILLIAM TINDALL

He was a joiner and lived at what is now 'Wroxton', Front Street, Hutton, and carried on his trade there until he died in 1931. When his father took over the business is not quite clear, but he was a joiner at Hutton in 1879. He doesn't seem to have been a native of Hutton Cranswick. The joiner's shop is still intact. In it was a circular saw turned by a handle. The power was supplied by Bill Tindall and his wife. When he died in 1931 the business finished, though his two sons carried it on for a short while from premises next door.

THE DOSSORS

The relations of the late Miss Elsie Dossor say that she told them she could trace their ancestors in Cranswick back to the fourteenth century when the village consisted of a few mud huts on the Green. Miss Elsie Dossor passed away not so long ago and any evidence of her ancestors living at Cranswick may have gone with her. We are on safer ground with Robert Dossor, born 1780, at Hutton Cranswick. At the time of the 1851 census he was an agricultural labourer and annuitant. His son Robert was a tailor. Arthur Dossor was a grocer in Cranswick until his death in 1931. The business was then run by his two daughters until it was taken over by Mr T. Megginson during the Second World War. The descendants of Robert Dossor are still living in Hutton Cranswick today.

CHAPTER TWENTY-SEVEN

HUTTON CHURCH AND ITS BELLS

The following extracts are taken from the Parish Magazine, July 1909:

The Patronage of Hutton Cranswick

The Church was given by Joan, wife of Gilbert Gertrude to the Priory of Watton, to which it was appropriated, and a vicarage ordained there on 18 December 1302. The patronage of the benefice originally was vested in the Crown, and the rectory seems to have passed from the Crown at the end of the reign of Queen Elizabeth to the Cromptons and Morehouses, and since the Reformation to the Hothams. The income of the benefice was at one survey only £40 a year and in 1818 £53.1s.0d. For a period there was no resident Rector as the report states, 'no minister', nor will the means support one. The tithe, which was originally to maintain the resident vicar amounts to £182 a year, but this had passed into lay hands, and the present vicar only receives £16 a year. You will all have seen in the newspapers the announcement that Lord Hotham has most generously handed over the Patronage for ever to His Grace, the Archbishop of York, and his successors. The present and all future vicars of Hutton Cranswick will have every reason to be grateful to his Lordship for his kindness and generosity, as the Ecclesiastical Commissioners have consented to augment the living to £200 a year.

Hutton Church Bells

The silver toned bells in our old Parish Church which week by week call the faithful to come to God's House and worship Him, and remind the careless of a duty they too often neglect, have a romance connected with them, if tradition may be relied upon. Perhaps it is no exaggeration to say that there is no village church in the district with sweeter toned bells than ours. They are supposed to have been founded originally for the Parish Church of Great Driffield, but never arrived so far. Probably disturbances were taking place which caused them to be placed in this tower for safety, and thus have remained there ever since. The bells were founded by Samuel Smith of York, from whose foundry bells were made for both the Minster and St Mary's Church at Beverley. The largest bell has the date 1635 with a Latin inscription which means 'Glory to God, Peace to Men'. The second bell, 1678, 'Glory in the Highest'. The smallest bell, 1678, 'Come, let us worship the Lord'. These bells, which for well nigh three hundred years have rung joyously at weddings and solemnly told the passing away of souls from this world to the veil within, each week call us to worship Almighty God, before whom we all must appear. May we not neglect our duty.

(Rev. Wheatley)

These three bells were taken down and recast in 1949 during the incumbency of the Rev George Storer, as they had lost that sweet tone the Rev. Wheatley had found so pleasing.

Of the other three, one is the Farmer's Bell. The second is in 'Memory of Jesse Barker, sexton until his death in 1924, and his wife Frances'. The third is in memory of the two children of Bob Severs of Highfield who were killed in an air raid, 18 - 19 March 1941.The bells were dedicated in July 1950 when the late W. Sissons represented the farmers.

CHAPTER TWENTY-EIGHT

CHARACTERS: TALES FROM THE PAST

There were many queer characters in this village. Eccentric seems a mild term for them. Most of the people mentioned here lived in the early part of this century and are part of our unrecorded history. They have vanished as the rural dweller became more sophisticated and moulded into one pattern as various Governments regulated his life from the cradle to the grave. Radio and television have also played their part.

One of these eccentrics was a chap called George Railton who lived in Southgate. Nicknamed 'Hotcakes', he was a bachelor and rented an acre or two of land from the Parish Council. He engaged someone to cultivate it and when asked what he was going to sow it with said 'Ah just fallus it. If ah saws it ah allus losses money at it'. He invested most of his money in the local public houses and came home one night full of ale. The next day he was found by the local policeman laid behind the door dead. The Coroner's verdict was 'Asphixiated while intoxicated'. His neighbours would say he 'slockened', this meant being choked.

One man was a professional 'caff', chaff carrier, and followed the threshing sets round the district in the winter time. When the parishioners' cows grazed the lanes he was one of the 'cow tenters'. This was only a summertime job and though he was only paid a few shillings a week it fitted in well with his winter caff carrying. On a threshing day this was the only job he ever did or could do. As this was the dustiest and dirtiest task to be found, he didn't get anybody trying to take the job off him. Once he walked a good five miles to a farm to carry caff on a threshing day starting at seven o'clock in the morning. When he arrived the farmer said 'Ah think we ev plenty o' men', though he had no intention of sending him away. The caff carrier said 'Ah can bloody well walk back', and turned round and walked the five miles home.

He was a bachelor and lived with his sister and her husband who once yoked up a horse and cart to meet him after a threshing day three miles away. They met about half way, but Frank, the caff carrier turned 'orkerd' and wouldn't get in the cart. Instead he walked the rest of the way home. The language which passed between them is quite unrepeatable. All this did not happen in the last century; it was in the 1930s. Today no one would ever dream of getting up at four o' clock in the morning and walking a few miles to work for eight shillings a day. All he would need to do would be to call at his local Social Security Office, where he would be allowed sufficient money to live on. Neither would he have to walk to collect it: if his case was thought deserving enough he might be allowed a taxi with the fare paid by the State.

Coultas Wilson, usually called 'Cowt', had a bit of land but was not a very successful farmer. He had a poor crop of oats bordering on a stream and one of the local wits said to him, 'Thoo wants ti gan doon ti them wots. Them frogs is gotten all'd boddem uns. Noo thur stanning on thur hind legs and earting 'd top uns'. He lived at the east end of Cranswick below the station and towards the end of his life was a cow tenter. For this he received nine shillings a week. He died before the First World War and seemed to have no kith or kin. All his furniture and effects were sold by auction. An old decrepit chair was held up by the auctioneer's assistant and a considerable number of gold coins fell out. The sale was stopped, though nobody knows what happened to the treasure trove. If any relative were found they would have benefited from the old man's thrift.

Another eccentric was a pillar of the little Methodist Chapel in Back Street, Hutton. Once during one of his prayers in the Service he finished with the sentence 'Tha knows Lawd wimmin likes soft watter ti wesh wiv'. Another time when the Preacher announced a hymn he said 'We arn't gooin ti hev that'. The Preacher, however, was equal to the occasion and said 'Thoo's nowt to dae wiv it. A'hs i charge ere'. That settled the argument. Dick, our old timer, also had a bit of land and would think nothing of digging a couple of acres even when well on in his sixties. I remember him once talking of a man in Hutton who farmed about thirty acres and one winter dug a nine acre field. I can't remember the name of the man or why he did it. He would most certainly have some draught animals though they may have been lame or laid up for some reason. At any rate Dick said, 'He nivver learked up frev his diggin till Nannie shooted dinner'.

Robert Barnes, Black Bob, lived at Chalk Pit Cottage Hutton. I can just remember him before the First World War gathering 'hoss muck' in an old pram. It must have been for his garden and he would be an old man then as he died in 1912 aged 81. At one time he kept a boar pig in the house and no one ever found out what happened to it. It may have ended up as bacon. He once said to a neighbour after killing a pig: 'Ahs gooin ti start at yan end and d'ord lass at tother an war gooin ti eart till wa meet'. He was certainly no weakling and in his younger days once carried a bag of potatoes, 8 stones, from Skerne to Hutton. That is about two miles. The only time it came off his back was when he put it on a gate post at Hutton railway crossing. He was once asked to bring an 18 stone bag of maize from Cranswick Station to a house at the back of the Green, a distance of nearly half a mile. He carried it all the way on his back.

He and another man named Parker were once engaged by Jonathan Dunn to mow a field of peas. That field now belongs to the Parish Council and is just over 27 acres. The crop was 'owerend'. That meant it wasn't battered down and Black Bob said. 'We'll goo right roond it'. No one knows how long it took them to go round the field the first time, nor how long it took to mow it. No doubt Black Bob would have a good supply of beer handy to refresh the inner man. He would certainly need it. He and his partner would have the mowing by 'tak', which meant they would be doing it for an agreed sum per acre. This would be only a few shillings as the farm workers wage at that time was only 15s. for a six-day week. Another case of 'by the sweat of thy brow'.

Another Bob was what was called a 'romancer'. He could also be described as a teller of tall tales. Once hearing a flock of wild geese flying over the house he said 'All adnt tarm ti ger outside, sae ah shuved mi gun up'd chimner an let go wi beath barrels. Oor Mary went ootside an gathered up a cloes baskit full a geese'. Another tale of his was how, when he heard the fox hounds coming his way in full cry after a fox, he loaded his old muzzle loader gun with a six inch nail and when the fox got abreast of him he fired the nail through its tail and pinned it to a wooden outbuilding. What he did with the fox nobody knows.

In the early part of this century there was a queer old character (I can't remember his name) who used to break stones on Cranswick Green in front of the shop, now a hairdresser's salon. It was then in the occupation of Mr Milner. His name can still be seen on the west wall facing up the Main street. The stone breaker was a short-tempered individual and if a stone didn't break he used to swear and hammer away viciously. The stones used to fly across the road towards the shop windows like rifle bullets. They escaped being broken with a few near misses. The stone breaker must have had a scientific approach to his job as he used to say 'It's shock at diz it'.

Dick Wilson, always known as Policeman Wilson, was the village policeman from 1910 until he retired in 1925. He was by no means a bully, but he often gave wrongdoers short shrift. As one Cranswick resident said, 'He used ti slounge (thrash) them ord harvesters'. These were the Irishmen who came to work on the farms for the duration of harvest. The policeman always carried what was called an 'ash plant'. This was a stout ash stick which could be used as a walking stick and also for administering corporal punishment. The harvesters often felt it across their backs if they were causing a row after the pubs turned out. This was a far better way than hauling them before the local magistrate. This often meant walking with an offender three miles to Driffield.

One man Dick was taking there insisted on walking on top of the gutter bank most of the way. Once, rather than go through all this with another offender he asked the man whether he would take his punishment on the spot or go before the magistrate. He decided he would have it there and then and got a good hiding with the trusty ash plant.

Jimmy Blanchard worked and lived in at Watton Abbey Farm then occupied by a man named Coulson. He was a good worker and remained with Coulson for many years. Periodically he went on the booze and though quite harmless, sometimes made a bit of a nuisance of himself. This happened once in Cranswick after the pubs had turned out. Dick Wilson decided to remove him. This is how he told the story. 'A'h thowt ahd tickle him up a bit sae ah got beyont im wi mi stick. By we'd gotten tid Wesleyan Chapel we wor in a canter; when we got ti'd High Road we wor off full gallop. He cudn't get tonned for Watton an went wrang roard ti Thriffield. Last a'h saw of im he was gooin helter skelter for Broach Hill'. A couple of days later the foreman from Coulsons asked Dick Wilson if he had seen Jimmy. He said he didn't know where he was. However, the missing man turned up safe and sound, a sadder and wiser man.

Before coming to Cranswick, Dick Wilson was stationed at Hunmanby and there was one village on his beat where some of the local farm lads were making a nuisance of themselves; they kept appearing at the windows of one of the little chapels and annoying the worshippers.

Some of the congregation told Dick and he promised to see to it. This was in the dark months of winter and the chapel backed on to a field. Like a true strategist he decided to catch them from the rear and walked across the field. Some of the lads were at the windows shouting 'Praise the Lord'. Dick shouted 'Amen', and brought his trusty stick down on as many as he could reach before they made off. This was the end of that problem. We could do with a bit of that kind of summary justice today.

Dick Wilson was also a great cricketer and played for the Hutton Cranswick team before and after his retirement. In Coronation Week, 1953, at the age of 76, he took part in a comic cricket match on the Green along with his youngest son, Laurie, and his grandson, John. He scored three. In the last years of his life he lived with his daughter at Lowthorpe where he died at the age of 86.

When Dick retired in 1925, The Chief Constable of the East Riding was Percy Sillitoe, later Sir Percy. He occupied that office from March 1925 to May 1926 aqnd even in that short period instituted many reforms. I remember one policeman who served under him saying 'Ord Sillitoe was a policeman's friend'. He learnt his policing in South Africa and Rhodesia where he rose from the ranks. When he left the East Riding he went to Sheffield where he crushed the razor gangs. Later, as Chief Constable of Glasgow, he stamped out war between the gangs and other undesirable elements. He was head of M15 from January 1946 until August 1953 and was the only policeman ever to hold that post.

It is not quite true that they were 'all straightforward English countrymen'. Some of them could be quite devious, as the following story shows. Arthur, usually known as Art, was a farmer who spent more time propping up public house bars than farming. Joe was a bachelor who never had a regular job. In winter he went 'tramp threshing' and in summer he did a bit of turnip hoeing, haymaking and harvesting. In his younger days, like many more casual workers, he went to what they called 'hay counthree'. This was Skipton, Grassington and district, where they used to mow all the grass with scythes. When it got to be hay, it was put into big cocks to withstand the weather. When this was finished Joe came back to his native parish ready for the harvest. His needs were few, he had only himself to keep. He also backed horses when he had enough funds to do so. One day he called at the Eagle Inn, Skerne, as he walked from Driffield to Hutton (he never rode a bike). While telling the landlord he had backed a certain horse with a bookmaker in Driffield, Art arrived and overheard. He also had just come from Driffield and knew the horse had won at favourable odds. Thinking that Joe didn't know his horse had won he offered to buy the bet from him, and Joe agreed. Art rushed to Driffield in his horse and trap only to find Joe had already collected the money.

A party of men, mainly from Cranswick, decided to emigrate to Canada. This was before the First World War. They didn't stay long as for some of them the boozer was too far away. One of them who was something of a wit indulged in a bit of leg pulling when he got back home. Knowing that most of his neighbours and the people he worked with had never been on a ship in their lives, he told how the Captain, whom he described as a first-rate seaman, 'Used ti sail'd'ord ship on top like a duck when it wus fine. If'd sea wus rough e used ti stick er right in sea sha wadn't blaw ower'.

CHAPTER TWENTY-NINE

THE EAST YORKSHIRE DIALECT

All the people in the preceding chapter would speak in what is called 'Broad Yorkshire'. That was the way they always spoke. They had learned it at their mother's knee and to a stranger it was like another language. Writing it is also a difficult matter. Words are put down as they sound. Most of them are connected with the soil or animals, are earthy, straight to the point and very much part of village life. Many of them are from Scandinavia; some are found in English Medieval verse.

'Arv' and 'gee' are used when driving horses; 'arv' means to go to the left and 'gee' to the right. Some horsemen said it didn't make any difference when driving a horse whether you used these words or not, yet many in the hands of a good horseman could be driven in the field with very little use of the 'plough strings', reins. 'Rax' is to stretch; an animal which is 'raxing' is said to be in good health. 'naup' means hitting someone over the head with a stick. A 'skeel' calf was one which was still getting milk. Up to the 1920s this description was used in auctioneers' sales adverts.

'Skelbea's' is the partition between horses or cows in the stable or cowhouse. I remember a vet once giving an injection to a cow tied to the 'skelbea's': he must have caught her unawares as she 'bealed oot' and shot through the open cowhouse door into the foldyard dragging the 'skelbea's' with her. 'Bealed oot' means bawling. A 'heck' is a rack which was filled with hay for horses, cows or bullocks. Anyone left-handed is 'gallic handed'. 'Fauf' means fallow. Before the tractor age there were specially made harrows with long straight teeth called 'fauf' harrows'.

'Cobbletree', more often called 'kibbletree', is the wooden crosspiece to which the swingletrees are attached, and to them the horses traces were fixed for ploughing, harrowing and practically all land cultivation. Many people born in East Yorkshire will have never heard of 'fire helding' (firewood). To 'snape' anybody is to snub them.

If you 'skime' at anybody you look at them sideways in a shifty manner. 'Soamy' means dopey. A 'stee' is a ladder. 'Slape' is slippery. To 'late' something is to seek it. A 'scopperil' is a teetotum. The last time I heard this word was during the last war by an old man in a blacksmith's shop. He once had an unwelcome visitor and told of how he got rid of him. 'This fella wuz cuming in every neet an oar missus sez thoo let ti get rid of im. Sae e cum i next neet an ah got'd poker and shoved it id fire. Than ah pulled it oot and felt at it. Ah did this a few tarms and e asked ma what a'h was deein it for. Ah sed when a'h ger it yat eneorf as 'ha gooin ti shuv it right up thi ... E wuz up an off like a scopperil'.

'Sad' has nothing to do with sorrow. Land which is heavy, wet and nearly impossible to work down in spring is said to be 'sad'. It also applies to cakes and other comestibles which haven't turned out right and are on the heavy side.

A man and a woman had lived all their lives in Hutton Cranswick and were distant relatives who bore the same name. The man was a little fattish chap who always seemed to have a baggy trousers behind. It was said he couldn't get through the churchyard kissing gate. He said to the woman, 'Thoo's been callin me a bag-arsed bastard'. After they exchanged a few insults she said, 'Thoo isn't a ..., thoo es ower monny farnticles on tha'. 'Farnticles' were freckles and that is the only time I have ever heard that word used.

'Steppen' is another dialect word I have heard only once. This was when my father related a story of a farmer who engaged a man to broadcast some corn. 'Steppen' meant rhythm, and as anybody knows who has used this method of sowing, the legs and arms must work in unison. The farmer showed the man where to start; he made a mess of it after a few steps, then said 'Diz thoo knaw maister ah clean forgottn'd steppen on it'. Maister said. 'Thoo niver knew it an thoo'd bether be off'. Broadcasting was the earliest form of sowing and old pictures always showed the sower using one hand. In this district both hands were used for sowing, with the exception of soot. Four yards were covered one way and four back. With clover or grass a slightly less 'breade' (breadth) was taken. This was a fairly sharp method of sowing provided the sower's feet and legs didn't give out. If he was walking over arable land with a lot of 'clots' (lumps) it was hard going. The last method of broadcasting, before it went from the rural scene, was for the sower to sit or stand on the back of a tractor-drawn trailer and throw fertiliser out behind. This wasn't a very accurate method of sowing and was never used for corn or grass.

Sowing soot was done quite differently. Up to the First World War, and even just after, a lot was spread on wheat in winter or early spring and always seemed to have a good effect. Today scientists tell us there is nothing much of value in it. Sowing soot was in a class by itself. The ordinary man on the farm hardly ever touched it; nor did he want to. The soot sowing was usually done by just a few men, sometimes a sweep or two among them. They would take it by the acre at an agreed price and stick at it until they finished it. This often meant living rough and not washing for a few days. The method of sowing was filling a big basket and throwing the soot down wind with one hand. Even so they got as black as any sweep, so much so that one farmer told his soot sower, 'Ah in't gooin to ha thoo i'd hoose. Thoo's like a damned greart chestnut hoss. Thoo let ti sleep i'd barn'. You would have thought he would have been more like a 'black hoss'.

A surly person is said to be 'juntas'. In the days when there was much home cured bacon about, if it went 'off' a bit it was said to be 'reasty'. It had a kind of monkey nut flavour and didn't taste so bad if not too far gone. The only thing to do was to get it eaten up as soon as possible. Horses that were bad pullers were said to be 'rearsted'. This was a bad fault and of some it was said, 'Tha wadn't pull an ord hen off its nest'. I remember one man watching his son mowing corn and saying, 'That lad sags at arse 'waintly', which means greatly. A person using some droll expressions is said to 'hae sum rum spaks'. 'Litha, litha, luxtha' means 'look here', and I have never heard it used since my schooldays. 'Skeg'd'ee' is still sometimes heard and means visual sighting and not taking exact measurements. One man who was often talking about doing things by this method fell off a stack. Nobody bothered much about him and as he was staggering home an acquaintance said, 'Is thoo gooin bid Skeg o'd ee, Martin'. Martin would have had a day or two off without benefit of a doctor and would be back at work again.

'Lillilow' is a light; 'Wezzin' is the windpipe; 'Warsle' is to wheedle and a 'theaker' is a thatcher.

Much of the thatching went after the First World War. Even though wages were only ninepence an hour from 1921 until the Second World War 'theaking' corn stacks was becoming too slow and costly, so 'theaking wi'd forrk' as it was called, came into being. To do this the stacks were not 'rigged up'. They were left flatter and then covered with a load of loose straw. Then a stack net was pulled over the lot to keep it from blowing away. If done properly this kept the stacks dry, though often it was hard to distinguish between corn and straw stacks as they both looked equally untidy.

'Staggarth' (stackyard) is of Scandinavian origin. The stacks have been gone for over a decade and often the only things in a stackyard are abandoned implements and a corn drier.

'Runnin teem forr' is an expression which is really of the horse plough days. It is mainly applied to ploughing and means running the plough in the 'forr' (furrow) without turning any soil over. This is for straightening the ploughing or running 'garings' off.

To go 'swint' across a field means going at an oblique angle. 'Quarting' is to plough a field for the second time across the furrows.

A plough mouldboard is a 'slipe'; a cap peak is a 'flipe'; a 'creark' is a crook; a 'stee' is a ladder; to 'bassock' anybody is to give them a hiding; 'Smopple' is something which is easily broken; 'tearf' is tough; a 'stowp' is a post; 'bearts' are boots; 'yan' is one; 'fowr' is four.

A ploughman ploughing deep is said to be 'stevvenin' it up' or 'sammin' it up'. If an East Yorkshireman says he is 'starved' it means simply that he is cold.

'Mormy' is sticky; when land is said to be 'clum' it means it is difficult to work. This often happens on heavy clay land after a wet winter. Manure, or 'fordyard muck' is called 'mannor'; 'manishment' is fertiliser.

A lighted candle where the flame is disappearing fast due to a draught is said to be 'swearling' away. Anyone who has had to use candles during power cuts will know what this means.

To 'steggle' means walking in an awkward manner and applies to both humans and animals; a drunk rolling along is said to be 'stegglin aboot'.

To 'spearn' is to wean; this usually applies to foals

Anyone in a 'fullock' is in a hurry. Anyone who is said to be 'allus rarving thur guts oot' is always hard at work and has no time for anything else.

To 'swizzen' is to burn or scorch; in the 1976 summer crops were said to be 'swizzened up'.

'Sleastering' is walking fairly sharp with slouching gait; holding anything is 'hoddin' it; anyone who is ill is said to be 'dowly'; to 'bawther' is to wander; 'yocken' means gulp.

This brings to mind the tale of the two men who were sharing a bottle of beer. The first one was to drink until he 'yockened'. As the beer kept going down his throat as if it was a sink the second man said, 'Thoos a lang tarm afoor tha yockens'.

A 'fussock' is a donkey; that word is no longer heard. A 'roark' is a mist. A 'jyster' is a heifer or bullock; usually store stock, taken in from May to October for summer grazing. This is derived from 'agistment', the taking and feeding of other men's cattle.

To give anybody a 'bensiling' is to give them a hiding; if anyone is said to have some 'mailocks' with themselves, it means they are getting in a muddle. It also applies to frisky animals. They could also be said to be 'stoddy', especially if they were hard to control.

A plough was often called a 'plearf'. When corn was tied up by hand the bands were made of corn stalks and one of the ways of fastening the ends together with one twist instead of several was known as the 'wauld wap'. It often came loose.

An expression used to describe some happening or event of no account was 'it wus like'd wind at blew ten year sen'.

A 'cauf' is a calf; a gusty, swirling wind is said to be 'gooarlin'.

'Loaunce' is the refreshment given midmorning and midafternoon on farms. Once it was only given during harvesting and threshing by the hinds who were allowed a little extra money for it. On the smaller farms the farmers' wives looked after it. Up to the middle 1920s a barrel of beer would be bought from the local brewery depot for harvest. All men, or lads, were supposed to have their mugs filled twice at 'loaunce tarm'. One foreman (the foremen always 'bulled oot', poured out) used to say, 'Es ivierybody ad od twice', then without waiting for any replies downed any beer that was left. Though beer was cheap and took little preparing, tea became the only drink supplied.

'Yam' means home; 'clunthering' is clumping; 'chunthering' is grumbling; 'mintin' at anything is to make ineffectual grabs at it; a 'mawk' is a maggot; a 'yow' is a ewe; a sheep which is laid fast on its back is said to be 'rigwelted'; to 'toam ower' is to faint.

'Frozzen' is frozen; a schoolboy crawling unwillingly to school with his hands in his pockets and his back up would be sometimes told 'Thoos like a dish a frozzen meart'.

'Conny' is small; 'splawther fearted' is splay footed; to be 'mafted' is to be overcome by heat; 'kessened' is christened; to 'lowp' is to leap.

In popular usage the word 'stunt' usually means something which catches the public eye and hits the headlines of the national press. In the vernacular of East Yorkshire it means a person who cannot be deterred from a certain course of action whatever the consequences. Someone who is stubborn. An animal which digs its feet in and refuses to move is said to be a 'stunt so-and-so'.

Cows which developed udder trouble were said to have 'segged'. This is mastitis. A vet new to the area often wondered what his client was talking about. A 'cuddy' is a hedge sparrow. A small boy is sometimes called that.

A 'barrfin' is a horse collar; a 'tearfitt' is a plover; a 'prickyochan' is a hedgehog; a 'moldywarp' is a mole; a 'smootole' is a small hole or hiding place, not, necessarily a mousehole.

'Kitlins' are kittens; a 'kearl pot' was a large iron cooking pot which hung over the old fashioned fire places on an adjustable arm called a 'reckon'; 'laikin' is larking; human feet which are hot and blistered are said to be 'scawthered'.

Chilblains were at one time just called 'frost i yer feet'. Pre-First World War schoolchildren, boys more than girls, often hobbled to school with their feet at all angles. It was painful but when spring and warmer weather came it disappeared and left no permanent disability.

A shooting day is always a 'shuttin' day. This also could lead to confusion, as when a member of the Women's Land Army was told by a farmer that he had just 'shutten' a pig, she thought he had shut it up in a building. When she found out it had been shot to be cured for bacon, she wasn't very pleased and said 'Why didn't the silly bugger talk proper?'

There are many more words and expressions which belong to the countryside of East Yorkshire. In the towns they were and still are out of place simply because they described the animals, the husbandry, the earth and the everyday life of the tiller of the soil. Even in an East Yorkshire town an employer would be staggered if a prospective employee said, 'Can thoo give us a job, Gaffer?' In the country that wouldn't matter so much provided he was the right man to fill the post.

'Arv' and 'gee' are heard no more because the horses have all gone. As have 'cobbletrees' and swingletrees'. Yet the mouldboard of a plough is still called a 'slipe' and the share a 'sock'. Some of the dialect has disappeared as farming has become more scientific.

Even in the 1930s corn which had ripened prematurely was said to have 'neet riped'. Most farmers thought this was caused by flashes of summer lightening during the night. It has since been proved that this was a disease called 'take all'.

The generation, or generations, which never knew radio or television spoke pure unadulterated East Yorkshire. Today it is more of a hybrid as modern usage creeps in. But it will never die out so long as the ploughman sets a 'rigg' across a field, 'bid skeg'd ee' and 'coos cleg' and bullocks 'bearl'.

CHAPTER THIRTY

REQUIEM FOR A VILLAGE

There the boys in summer days played cricket
And whacked the ball into the thicket.
There the calves first turned out in June
Galloped as if to jump o'er the moon.

And Tom and Blossom pulled the old grass reaper
When the hedges were festooned with creepers.
There in pre-baler days we forked the hay
As if there would never be another sunny day.

The calves, the cricket, and the rest have gone,
Instead,, there are houses, with all mod. and con.
In summer where the old cows used to 'bawther'
There is nothing now but bricks and mortar.

In harvest where the old binder used to clatter
(The crops we grew no longer matter),
The only things that sprout are signs 'For Sale'
It is bricks and cement instead of kale.

There we knocked apples from the trees,
With thoughts of schoolday's end and we'd be free.
And in those fields in harvest holidays.
dreamed the dreams of childhood days.

The field where Tom Arnell used to swing 'd'ord ley'
And cut and shake the grass up into hay,
The land where he used to 'rarv and tew'
Is now just called Laburnum Avenue.

Down the roads where the lane cows used to wander
(They graze the verges and the banks no longer)
It is by no means safe to stay and ponder
As you may get hit by a Mini or a Honda.

Gone the pumps where we lifted water from the earth
With sweat, swear words and muscle straining jerks.
We no longer watch the summer skies for rain
As we have water metered from the mains.

Over the old privies we'll discreetly draw a veil
And say they are definitely beyond the pale.
The village they certainly did not enhance,
to them we'll merely say, 'Good riddance'.

Now the people too are changing fast,
And where the joiner plied his ancient craft,
Or where the cobbler beat leather on his last
There often resides a minor bureaucrat.

Over a thousand years this place has stood
But its rural image has now gone for good
It can't be called proud town or village mean
It is just a poor and gaudy in-between.

At the present time in Hutton Cranswick there are:

2 joiners and builders; 3 garages; 2 grocers shops; 1 butcher; 1 builder; 1 joiner; 1 welding and construction specialist; 1 agricultural contractor; 1 fried fish shop.

These could be said to be following their trades like the blacksmiths, joiners, etc., of the previous century, except that they are using equipment unthought of by the craftsmen of that age. What was once a grocer's shop is now a ladies' hairdressing emporium. Up to the First World War a 'hairdresser' was a barber who cut the men's hair. Often he was one of the tradesmen who did this as a sideline and there being no dictates of fashion he just chopped the hair off as short as possible

There is also one mill, a chemical spray depot, and a few other industries on the old airfield just outside Cranswick village. One seed cleaning and dressing plant in what was once a sack depot. It was originally built by the War Department in 1939 and since extended. Also, typical of the age in which we live, a firm working in plastics in the Cranswick Station buildings.

The Hutton Post Office closed on 13 April 1977, after being in business for most of this century. All the business was transferred to Cranswick. The village band which had performed successfully for many years was disbanded during the early years of the Second World War and was never reformed. The cost of instruments to equip a band today would be a staggering figure. The Football Club is still going strong. After being out of commission for a few years the Cricket Club is now functioning again. The Tennis Club, formed in the early 1920s, also folded up a number of years ago.

In 1949 building started on the Hotham Road Council houses. There were approximately 39 and this was the first building scheme of any size in the village, with the exception of the few built on the Hutton Road in 1925. As far back as 1914 the Parish Council passed a resolution that houses should be built to relieve overcrowding. Thus after 35 years and several proddings by the Council, young people who couldn't afford a home of their own were offered modern accommodation. Even though a house could then be built for £2,000 to £3,000, it was out of the reach of many. There were some additions to this estate in later years.

There was not a great deal of building except for some private dwellings and the population remained about the same.

In the 'sixties and 'seventies the building really started with the speculator and the building developer moving in and erecting houses for all who were able to buy them. Hobman Lane, the old 'Oggleman', was built up. This road in most places was only the width of a cart and a large sum of money was spent on widening it.

Southgate, or 'Blathergate', had some house building inflicted on it. It is a narrow cul-de-sac and cannot be widened without a great deal of expense. A hundred odd houses were also built near the station and about the same number near the Beverley-Driffield Road.

The ordinary layman may wonder why in a straggling village nearly a mile and a half across, all those empty spaces bordering a good and fairly wide road should not be filled in. Such a solution is far too simple for any planner, and he would have some very plausible explanation as to why they allow building in some wet and inaccessible place. The Piper Field development in Back Street (Orchard Lane) Hutton, where 33 houses are being built, is on a higher and drier site, but the main approach road to it from the Beverley to Driffield road is one way. To make the roads which traverse the village wide enough to cope with all the modern traffic would cost a tremendous amount. No local authority is going to spend money to that extent.

Since Humberside was foisted upon us against the wishes of the majority of the inhabitants of East Yorkshire, we all pay the same rates. Here the rural areas are the losers, whilst the urban areas have better libraries, shopping facilities and transport. There must have been a tremendous increase in the amount of money paid by the ratepayers to the local authority in the last eighteen to twenty years, yet a request for an extra footpath, or even improving an old one, gets the reply, 'No money', but there always seems to be plenty of cash to spend in the Bridlington area to attract the tourists.

The only good thing about the new local authorities is that the Parish

Councils can now express their views on planning, where before they were just ignored. On second thoughts the situation is not so much different as the planners still go their own way.

Nowadays we have all kinds of people cultivating a rural image, from Cabinet Ministers downwards. Most of them gave the rural areas a wide berth during the era of pumps and privies; now they are moving into the country in increasing numbers.

Today, many more people can afford to enjoy that untaxable commodity, fresh air. The ordinary villager, the man whose roots may go back centuries, does not care a toss what the people around him get up to as long as they behave themselves and leave him alone. What he or she resents is the attitude of people who, as soon as they arrive here, write letters to the local press complaining about various things. Maybe the new arrivals think the locals need 'wakkenin up' a bit, or that a stranger on the scene can look at it from a different angle, which may be true.

The Driffield Times of 1 May 1975 reports on a parish meeting when there were many protests about a land development proposal in Piper Field, Back Street, Hutton. (No one knows the origin of the name Piper.) One resident wanted to know why the Parish Council had not objected when the houses to be built there were increased from 27 to 47. Another one described the plan as 'an abomination'. An action committee was also advocated to fight the proposal, and a planning officer who was present said they were being urged by the government to encourage higher density building developments.

Now we move on to 15 May, and the protesters, who had formed a Residents' Association. had also written to the local MP, Sir Paul Bryan, who supported them. In this letter several points were stressed:

> that a sixty per cent increase in the number of Hutton dwellings would alter the character of the village;

> that the present school in Cranswick is inadequate;

> there is no evidence of an unmet demand for housing in the parish of Hutton Cranswick;

> it would be outrageous if the outcome was to be the destruction of the 'village soul' in return for empty houses arising from high density building.

Another letter writer that same month had horrifying visions of gardens being uprooted and double yellow lines up and down the streets with perhaps a traffic warden round the corner. He could also see urban streets and urban footpaths. Today, most of the residents of Hutton who do any walking would be glad of any kind of decent footpath, urban or otherwise. The parish meeting referred to previously, which was more like a town demonstration, upset some of the old inhabitants because most of the protesters were unknown to them. Of course, like many villages, a man may have lived here for twenty years and still be a stranger, and the brash, talkative individuals are often treated with suspicion. The Yorkshire adage, 'See all, hear all, an say nowt', applies much more to the countryside than the town.

With great zeal the protesters took petitions round Hutton Cranswick village and an outlying portion of the parish. Rightly, or wrongly, the old timers said these people were merely trying to protect their own little bit of suburbia. Against this the protesters could have argued that no one had bothered about high density building development until they arrived. This may have been true to a certain extent, but at one time houses were needed to relieve overcrowding. Then building got out of hand and whether any group of people could have nipped the planners' schemes in the bud is doubtful.

The crusaders must have run out of steam later, as there were no murmurs of dissent when it was finally decided two years ago that the thirty-three houses to be built on the Piper Field site should be £20,000 and upwards. (Today the price could be nearer £40,000.) The Parish Council recommended that there should be some cheaper. There were sympathetic noises from the District Council but the scheme was passed unaltered. These prices put them out of the reach of the native people of the village, who must surely be the 'soul of the village', and not bricks and mortar.

There are also other houses in the £30,000 bracket. All this helps to make Hutton Cranswick just a commuters' dormitory, and it will get more so as long as these expensive houses continue to be built. Many of them would merge perfectly in the suburbs of a town; in this village they are just out of place.

All the shouting and tumult didn't halt the planning juggernaut and there has been limited building outside the sacred cow of a village plan. The conservation plans for the two areas are useless while the infilling building goes on there. At the moment the planners are resting from their labours and Hutton Cranswick has got a reprieve for the moment. The Parish Council has passed resolutions that all building in Hutton Cranswick should cease when the present planning phase ends. Most residents would agree with this as the population must be nearly 2,000. It will be interesting to see what the next census figures tell us.

This influx of people is helping to create two groups. On the one hand we have the indigenous villagers, on the other the new arrivals, most of them products of the towns. The first group live in the older parts of the village and the council houses, because not many of them can afford the expensive new ones. Most of the second group live in these expensive houses and will soon equal the other one in numbers. This also destroys village life and helps to create a kind of upper strata whereby the poor old villager's voice is drowned by those who are more articulate but who may not have more common sense. Those who shout the loudest can always get a good hearing whatever the merits of their case.

What of the future? It is said that oil may become very scarce in the next twenty to thirty years. Many kinds of disaster are predicted, though in the past many of these prophets of doom have been proved wrong. Will all fuel be severely rationed as in wartime and those posters asking 'Is your journey really necessary?' return? The Government of the day may curtail building in the country and compel houses to be erected in or near the towns where so many people work. Some of our present-day rulers are thinking along these lines. If all these things come to pass, this village may become a graveyard of suburban houses. Stranger things have happened in history.

One thing is quite sure, the individual who works the land will still be here whether there is any fuel or not. He may have to return to the ways of his forebears and go back to the horse or rely on his own muscles and the civil servants and form-fillers may have to accompany him. The mere thought of horses will send shivers down the spines of most agriculturalists, because they are so mechanised and dependent on oil. Most of them have become so used to riding everywhere that to use their legs and feet again would be like stepping back into the Middle Ages. There are said to be reserves of coal in this country to last 200 to 300 years, depending on how fast we use it up. It may be developed efficiently to take the place of oil in propelling all those machines on which modern civilisation depends.

Much of our countryside is man made, otherwise it would have remained a mass of scrub and just a wilderness. Yet one writer says there is very little to show where our ancestors and their animals laboured. This is hardly true. Witness the fields they enclosed, the hedges they planted, the ditches they dug and the land they drained. All was done slowly and painfully over the centuries with inadequate tools. This is their memorial. And when they came to the end of their days it was fitting that the soil, the earth, with which they had wrestled for a lifetime and which had given them their livelihood, should receive them gently.

CHAPTER THIRTY-ONE

POSTSCRIPT

In adding another chapter to Herbert Johnson's book I cannot pretend to have his knowledge of village history. However, having lived in Cranswick since 1977, I feel qualified to record the major changes to the two villages in the final two decades of the twentieth century. Throughout this period both villages have evolved. More new housing has appeared, especially in Cranswick, whilst new businesses have arrived and older ones have expanded.

One major area of expansion is the industrial estate on the old airfield. Twenty years ago the airfield was still being used by crop spraying biplanes. It was a common sight to see these aircraft hedge-hopping around the fields in this area. Nowadays the crop spraying is carried out at ground level by specially designed tractor-type vehicles. A crop spraying business is still based in the villages, having recently moved from Cranswick to Hutton, that move making way for Glenholme Court, a small development of bungalows and flats off Main Street.

The villages now consist of around 840 homes of one type or another. Most new housing having been built in Cranswick. The extension to Beech View and the addition of Oaklands and Ash Grove has added seventy new homes, a few being suitable for first time buyers. Another area which has seen considerable new housing development is Station Road and Sheepman Lane. Housing along Station Road and The Pastures replacing the milking sheds which stood there in the early eighties, whilst the old barn on the corner of Sheepman Lane has made way for Richmond Terrace. Keldgarth, down Sheepman Lane, has also replaced old farm buildings. In addition to these building projects, in-fill housing has appeared in virtually every area of Cranswick.

Hutton has seen some new building but not to the same extent as Cranswick. The Paddocks in Hutton Road and The Orchards in Orchard Lane have been the main developments. In-fill housing has also been completed in Howl Lane and Orchard lane. Planning applications are currently being considered for yet more housing, some of it in Hutton.

The introduction of a mains gas supply to the villages was welcomed by many residents. Other services which have seen improvements are street lighting and footpaths, whilst the travelling library has been replaced by the trailer library. The trailer standing in station yard for the whole of Monday. On the negative side we have lost the services of the village policeman. We do have policemen living in the villages but the village bobby has apparently gone forever. Thinking along those same lines, we have doctors living in the villages but no village surgery - despite our best efforts.

Another anomaly, which many find frustrating, is the business of car taxation. In the villages we can buy a new or used car from any of the four garages, we can have it repaired, serviced, mot'd and insured but, because of some bureaucratic nonsense emanating from Swansea, we cannot tax it at the village post office.

Good communications are essential for the maintenance of a thriving village community. Far too often nowadays one reads of villages losing their bus services, their shops and their post offices. In Hutton Cranswick we are fortunate to have a regular bus service as well as the rail service. Twice in the last twenty years winter snows have closed the roads out of the villages. However, on both these occasions the railway has kept running. I believe it is essential that the rail service is maintained and, if possible, expanded. Improvements in the rolling stock in use are becoming evident - trains of the trans-pennine type replacing the 'tin sheds on wheels' which until recently ran along our line. The introduction of the automatic level crossings at both Hutton and Cranswick led to the demolition of the signal box at the station and to the station becoming unmanned.

The growth in the population has seen the re-introduction of another form of road communication - the private hire taxi service. Busy B's service being established in Cranswick in the nineteen eighties. Earlier taxi businesses were closed down some years ago.

One family business, which moved from Hutton to Cranswick, has seen the emphasis of its business change from building to civil engineering. Simpsons civil engineers have expanded considerably in the last few years. Londesboro nurseries have expanded to include a garden centre. Two residential/nursing homes have been established. One local farmer has diversified by establishing a spring water bottling plant whilst another is running a 'books by post' scheme. The farm shop on the main road is also relatively new.

All the traditional trades are still here. The village has builders, plumbers, joiners, a roofing service, and a painter and decorator. The three public houses are still in operation, one having expanded to provide accommodation and a restaurant. There are two mini supermarkets, one of which now harbours the post office, a butcher, a fried fish shop and a hairdressers. A number of other small businesses are run from home. We also have the services of a mobile optician one half day per week.

Cranswick village green has seen a number of changes, the most recent being the demolition of the old school rooms. Now that the site has been levelled and grassed over it is hard to imagine that buildings ever stood there. Improvements were made to the children's play area which included new fencing to keep out dogs and the shrubbery which encircled the pond was removed because of the litter it collected. The other major change was the move by the cricket club from the green to the new site at the corner of Meggison's Turnpike.

At one stage in the not too distant past it seemed that everywhere you went groups or individuals were raising money in one way or another for the Sports and Recreational Association. All that effort culminated in the magnificent facilities that are now available in Rotsea lane. Football, cricket, tennis and even fishing - no doubt there are other sporting facilities there as well. Not that the sporting facilities are restricted to Rotsea lane, the Bowls club are centred in Cranswick as are the keep fit classes.

There are many other groups and organisations centred on St Peters church, the Chapel, the school and the W.I. and Foresters Halls. The Bulletin, the Hutton Cranswick newsletter continues to be published on a monthly basis and contains news of forthcoming events from many of the village organisations. The number and variety of all these clubs and organisations are an indication to me of a thriving community.

Hutton and Cranswick, or Hutton Cranswick if you prefer it that way, have expanded since nineteen eighty. Changes have occurred which have no doubt upset some people but, overall, the impression I have is of a healthy, developing community. I am happy living here and pleased to be back in East Yorkshire.

Leslie Wilkie
October 1999.

Two Further views of Cranswick Station around 1900.

Mill Street, Hutton, from Back Street (now Orchard Lane), looking south.

Orchard Lane, Hutton, before the bungalow and The Orchards were built.

Hempholme Locks in 1906.

Aerial view of Hutton before the Piper's Road development.

APPENDIX 1

TOWN & COUNTRY PLANNING

At the beginning of the 20th century the Parish of Hutton Cranswick had a population around the 1,000 mark. During the subsequent 70 years this increased by about 10%. The last 30 years have witnessed an escalation in population by 82% to the present figure of approximately 2,000. An overview of the planning process will help put this trend into perspective.

Town and Country Planning has a strong influence on present-day village life. Changes in the physical environment if not sensitively done reflect badly on all involved. Herbert Johnson represented many people's views in his criticism of the changing built form of Hutton Cranswick. Both villages bear the scars of poor planning decisions yet are still regarded as attractive places to live in.

The Town and Country Planning Act, 1947 was part of the radical reform of post-war Britain. It is enough to say that comprehensive powers were given to local authorities to plan and control "development" throughout the land. East Riding County Council was the local planning authority with certain delegated powers given to the Rural and Urban District Councils.

It was not until 1964 that the first local statutory plan, the East Riding County Development Plan was approved. Apart from the larger urban areas like Bridlington and Driffield certain villages were identified as being suitable for growth. Generally they were the larger villages with adequate services and educational facilities. In planning jargon they were "minor centres", where all suitable development was to be encouraged. Hutton Cranswick was such a place.

The 1947 Act had contained urban sprawl but was not refined enough to prevent a wave of unsuitable development in existing settlements. Just look along Hutton Road to judge this statement.

By 1972 a village plan was prepared. An increase of population from 1,155 to 1,630 was anticipated as was a scheme for the disposal of sewage to cater for a population of 2,140. The plan described the two villages as being capable of accommodating a moderate increase in population. In Hutton the plan scheduled three areas: what is now Piper Close, land immediately south of Church Lane and land off Orchard Lane. In Cranswick two large areas were zoned: the Londesborough Road estate and Laburnum Avenue/ Sycamore Close.

The rapid implementation of this plan brought widespread feeling in the villages against further development. It has been stated that too much happened too quickly under ineffective planning control. This reaction was reflective of national opinion, for planning like local government is under constant review through changing legislation taking in public pressure and the political climate of the day. The system was not getting it right.

To aid stability and environmental quality Conservation Areas were designated in Cranswick in 1976 and Hutton in 1977. These are areas for those parts of towns and villages which are considered as having a special character or appearance which it would be desirable to keep and improve. That in Cranswick centres on The Green whilst St. Peter's Church, a Grade II* Listed Building forms the nucleus for Hutton Conservation Area. In the list of Buildings of Special Architectural or Historic Interest of 1987 Hutton Cranswick has seven buildings included.

Re-organisation of local government in 1974 resulted in a two tier planning system with Humberside County Council mainly concerned with strategic matters and East Yorkshire Borough Council, (called at first North Wolds), with local planning functions. Humberside's Structure Plan, the strategic planning policy document, was approved in 1987, Hutton Cranswick becoming a "selected settlement," a similar status to the old "minor centre." It was stated that in certain circumstances a selected settlement could reach its planned size at populations of 2,000 and 4,000 inhabitants.

Pressures for development within the villages resulted in the Borough Council producing an Interim Policy Statement in 1987. It anticipated a rise in population from 1,724 in 1981 to 1845 in 1991 and calculating that 10-15 dwellings per annum would be needed over a 5-10 year period. A number of options were suggested for land to be developed.The results now form The Paddocks off Hutton Road, Keldgarth off Sheepman Lane and The Pastures off Station Road.

The unpopular Humberside County Council lasted little more than two decades to be replaced by the current unitary authority, East Riding of Yorkshire Council in 1996. By this time a replacement Structure Plan was adopted. It looked for some 12,400 new homes in the old East Yorkshire Borough area during the period 1991-2011. Specific allocation for land for these dwellings was part of the role of the current East Yorkshire Borough Wide Plan with land availability and public opinion weighing heavily in the selection process. As a result Hutton Cranswick fared quite well with 8.1 acres allocated for development in two areas of Cranswick, 2 acres being at Churchill Avenue and the rest East of Southgate, linking up with the existing estate development.

Throughout the 1990's the Parish Council had campaigned for the two villages to be regarded as having reached their planned size. The 8.1 acres were seen as rounding off development in Cranswick with no further support for expansion.

The turn of the 20th century will see a further review of Hutton Cranswick's suitability for change. A joint Structure Plan between the County Council and the City Council of Hull is taking place with much land needed for further residential development as a result of government population projections. With current government policy encouraging the use of public transport settlements benefitting from good road and rail links will be looked at closely.

It remains to be seen what role, if any, Hutton Cranswick has in a 21st century planning strategy for the region. Whatever the outcome, decisions will need to take account of any views expressed by the 2,000 or so people who live here.

Norman Smith
December 1999

SELECT BIBLIOGRAPHY

Works consulted by Herbert Johnson in the preparation of the first edition include:-

W.P. Baker, 'Parish registers and illiteracy in Yorkshire'. (East Yorkshire Local History Society)

Cobbett's Country Book

J.H. Fletcher 'The making of modern Yorkshire', 1750 to 1914. (East Yorkshire Local History Society)

K.A.MacMahon, 'The beginnings of the East Yorkshire Railways' (East Yorkshire Local History Society)

Rev. C.J.Morriss, 'Yorkshire Reminiscences'

D. Neave, 'Londesborough' (Londesborough Silver Jubilee Committee, 1977)

Pears Encyclopaedia

Pierepoint's autobiography

A.W.M. Stirling, 'The Hothams' (1918)

J.T.Ward, 'East Yorkshire Landed Estates in the Nineteenth Century'.

H Woodcock, 'Piety among the peasantry'

E.L.Woodward, 'History of England' (Methuen,1961)